FINDING YOUR SELF THROUGH MADNESS

NICKI HOLLAND

PS AVALON
Glastonbury, England

© Nicki Holland 2008

First published in the U.K. in 2008 by PS Avalon

PS Avalon
Box 1865, Glastonbury
Somerset, BA6 8YR, U.K.

www.psavalon.com

*Nicki Holland asserts the moral right
to be identified as the author of this work*

front cover design: Candy Holland

book design: Will Parfitt

All rights reserved. No part of this publication may be reproduced, sorted in a retrieval system, or transmitted in any form or by any means, electronic, mechanical, photocopying, recording or otherwise, without the prior permission of the publisher, except in the case of brief quotations embodied in articles and reviews.

ISBN 978-0-9552786-7-9

Finding Your Self Through Madness

Nicki Holland

Contents

Introduction	6
1. A Question of Madness	9
2. An Energy Beyond the Boundaries of the Body	19
3. A Spectrum of Light and Darkness	36
4. A Construct of Self	51
A: 'When I look I am seen, so I exist'	51
B: Self individuation or a self full of shame and fear	61
C: Seeking clarity	73
5. A Formation of Repeating Patterns	84
A: Reproducing our primary relationships and environment	84
B: Ongoing mind-body patterns	89
6. A Perspective of Madness and Sanity	103
A: Symptoms and defences, procedures and attitudes	103
B: Recognising our psychic disorders and defence mechanisms	113
C: Coming to our true senses	126
7. An Empowering or Disempowering Therapeutic Holding	139
A: Seeing what is needed	139
B: Discovering what it takes	147
C: A therapeutic rock or rocking	159
D: Hitting rock bottom	168
8. A Centre of Powerful Loving	179
9. An Emergence of Our True Self	192
Glossary	204
Bibliography	219

Introduction

What's madness but nobility of soul. At odds with circumstance?
Roethke,1975

We all have a touch of madness in us. Most people have the odd manic outburst, patch of *paranoia* and dose of *depression* and get away with it – but not everyone does. Some find medication alleviates such mental disorder while, for others, madness takes over. There is another way, however, of handling the crazy elements in our *psyche*.

Finding Your Self Through Madness gives an account of how we can weather a mental breakdown and come through with a more robust, real sense of *self*.

Whoever in their right mind would choose to explore madness? This book invites you to do just that. It challenges what are deemed to be normal standards of mental health and invites you to consider the benefits, and the dangers, of revealing what is deep within your unconscious. It is a demanding process as we are treading on delicate and potentially explosive ground. However, those of us who hide behind a public mask are the very people with the most to gain from confronting their mad elements. An extraordinary, bold and risky suggestion it may be, but one which is the foundation of this book.

While some rudiments of mental development are included as a framework to support you in this emotional venture, the perspective I present is not just from my objective viewpoint as a professional *psychotherapist* but also from my personal experience. Having a brush with madness is a very different story to the clinical theory.

Overall, Winnicott and Bowlby have provided the bedrock for child development studies, while I have needed Assagioli to be flanked by the founding fathers Freud and Jung, in exploring the need to 'grow down' (Hillman's term) before growing up. I borrow Bion's term of *non being* although what I have to say about it is original.

This personalised mix is pertinent as, when I was in the throes of *psychotic* episodes, most scholarly volumes lacked an essential ingredient. I was desperate for help from people who really knew what they were talking about, for themselves - and to me, the writers' words were not informed by an intimate connection to their own psychotic realm.

I do remember reading Brian Keenan's (1992) book, *An Evil Cradling*, and exclaiming with relief, 'Yes, that's how it is – he knows what it's like!' His experience of captivity and torture was fact, whereas mine was a creation of my imagination. However, where his world and mine converged was when the real danger to his physical survival waned and his psyche continued to play out his living nightmare in *hallucinations*. I felt the horror of what Keenan had endured coming from the pages of his book and such empathy rising within me for this man who had 'been there'. His words gave me precious comfort and heartening courage.

Of course, no one makes an identical inner journey or comes to the same conclusions. However, my greatest inspiration for writing this first hand account of psychological turmoil and recovery is that some who are troubled by their own, or another's, mental distress may feel a link with me as they read of my experiences.

Since the language I use is more commonplace than in academic literature, the material might also awaken an interest in those uninitiated in the capriciousness of the psyche. My intention is for all readers to be stimulated, in an exciting and meaningful way, by notions which may challenge their own. Indeed, this book offers an unusual twist to mental development in that it focuses on the potential creativity in psychological disturbance. Thus it may prove a source of candid communication provoking debate on madness - which by its very provenance is as abstruse and difficult to understand as it is disturbing.

I sincerely hope that presenting my view on this complex subject might further an understanding and tolerance of mental disorder and may evoke greater respect for those who seek to grow from their psychotic roots.

As it is, most of us fear madness. It is all too close for comfort - best not to think about it, let alone go there. Yet such defensive devices prevent us from discovering the many intrinsic resources which lie enmeshed within this much damned area of our psyche. It may be hard to believe but, in finding our way through madness, we can end up with what is a clearer and more healthy sanity than that considered the norm. Either we take a proactive step to embrace what is in our psychotic layer, or run the risk of these powerful *drives* breaking through for themselves when we are ill-prepared.

The most common and deepest urge in mankind, for those who feel in control of their life and others going through psychological disturbance, is the longing for someone to come close and really know them. If we explore our psychotic dimension with a person well acquainted with this area, the ultimate reward is that we may develop an intimate and loving relationship with our self and with others. We all yearn to be loved for who we genuinely are. Yet so many of us fear rejection if our deepest substance was to be revealed.

When in the grip of madness alone with our 'monsters', often we can but cling to a wall or hug a cushion. If this book speaks meaningfully to those trapped in this terrifying space and gives them a voice, then it has done its job. It further extends a hand of encouragement, not only to those who feel crazy, but to all whose defence against what lies at the root of their psyche means they feel that the life they are leading is precarious, inauthentic and unfulfilling.

So whether you are mindful of others' well being, you feel something missing in your life or you are wobbling on the tightrope of mental illness, you might find that an answer, not the answer, lies herein.

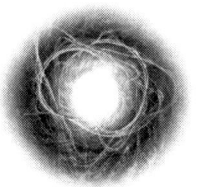

Chapter 1
A Question of Madness

Do you think you are mad?, the psychotherapist asked. Somewhat taken aback by his directness, I simply said, 'Yes'. 'Well then', he replied, 'you might not be. Had you answered "No" to my question then chances are, you are.'

This opening dialogue might remind you of one between Alice and the Mad Hatter. But when immersed in reading Lewis Carroll's story of *Alice's Adventures in Wonderland* did you not feel as Alice, *'that nothing surprised you'*. The therapist's words seemed no more bizarre than everything else that was happening to me at the time. In truth, until then, I had not associated my recent turns with madness. Extraordinary, yes. Horrifying, most certainly. But me, insane?

Come to think of it, was it madness to see monsters intent on annihilating me? Or, was I just scared out of my wits? But these apparitions had a palpable physical impact on me, so much so that my outside felt inside and my insides seemed outside. Even feather light movements, quite remote from me, would make me recoil as if to an electrical shock. Perhaps I was as mad as a hatter.

Symptoms like these can be neatly bound by the psychiatric terms *fragmentation* or *Post Traumatic Stress Disorder* 'P.T.S.D.' But when in the grip of such episodes the world, not oneself, appears fragmented and traumatic. While my symptoms did not mean I was suffering from a psychotic disorder such as *schizophrenia* or *bipolar affective disorder*, I was certainly experiencing psychotic episodes. *Psychosis* (used throughout the book as a broad-based term unless specified as psychiatric classification), occurs when we are swamped by the expansiveness of our perceptions, yet our reality bears little resemblance to what is apparent to others in the outside world.

'If you feel mad', the therapist went onto explain, 'then you have some objectivity, some sense of self in reality.' While in the moment I could not grasp the full significance of what he was saying, I found that I was to cling onto his diagnostic folderol for many years to come. This sliver of self awareness in psychological assessment terms would be listed as an *inclusion* factor. Was this enough to outweigh my serious *exclusion* factors such as being beset by hallucinations and an urge to self harm? As a psychotherapist myself, the theory of psychosis was familiar and made sense to me. However when it took all I could do to muster the strength to survive from moment to moment, the experience seemed unprecedented.

'Are you mad?' is a common, derisory put-down. But my therapist's question was deadly serious and my quick response important. It left me, however, immediately preoccupied by the possibility of being interned in a psychiatric unit. After all, anyone in the same room as me was a threat - but if they were to touch me … it was beyond the bearing. Just the idea was sufficient for me to conjure up 'real' figures coming to restrain me. Surely, while I might not be totally mad, what normal perceptions I had left were in jeopardy.

But my therapist considered that, with his help, I might win through without psychiatric intervention or drugs. Such crucial judgment can come from a professional's ignorance or an inflated *ego*. But I was lucky. This therapist's decision was fed by a deep knowledge and experience of psychosis. It demanded a huge commitment on his part. He knew that – but I did not.

At the time, I was too confused for any of this to register. I was oblivious to his assessment and its indications. Neither could I envisage the long challenging years which lay ahead during which I would have to struggle each day for my sanity.

Looking back, it seems very odd that, until my therapist asked the big question as to whether I thought I was mad, the possibility just had not occurred to me - but then there is not much room for logical associations when bordering on an indefinable crazy realm. Psychotic forces took me totally by surprise.

For that reason, I have opened my story by also plunging straight into these abysmal realms with little explanation as to what it is all about. However, after describing some psychotic episodes, which by their very nature have no *boundary*, we will dip in and out of psychological constructs. Theory offers a holding device for the amorphous material which is liberated in psychosis. Thus a more objective vantage point will be reached from which to view where I am coming from. We will find a way through the arena of madness and out the other side to a totally new vista.

It is hard to calibrate my journey in figures. My route fluctuated so widely. My timing was so twisted. But I reckon that during the first nine months I was more in than out of madness. Thankfully, over the next three years these trips became less frequent, extreme and of shorter duration. However, it was to be ten years before I felt a surety of my emergence from this psychotic world. Of course, some bits of my psyche still remain in this outlandish place. But now I can opt to just pop in for a brief visit during therapy, whereas when my psychosis first burst forth, there was no choice.

When you feel you are going mad, anything seems possible. Pigs might indeed fly! Let me tell you, TV villains can come out of the box to get you and dark trees really do have menacing faces and arms which reach out to grab you. Childhood fantasies become your reality.

But rather than meeting, like Alice, the fanciful White Rabbit or disembodied Cheshire Cat who could talk, even the Red Queen who would cut off heads at a whim, most of my hallucinations had a substantial, albeit *primitive* quality to them.

I remember the horrifying sensations of an 'iron maiden', a torturing device in olden times, closing tightly around my body and trying to force the very life out of me. No amount of reasoning, even now, can take this experience away from me. Somehow, I feel as if I have lived this, and died in this way.

One night, my bed became a coffin. Completely enclosed, the pressure on my body was unbearable. Then came total, smothering blackness as I was swallowed up into the bowels of the earth. In such appalling confinement I was riveted with fear. It was so real. I could not breathe. I really thought I was dying.

My house afforded no protection. Entities kept looming out from behind my settee and crashing through the doors and walls without warning. Once they appeared, nothing could stop their attack. How to escape from this torment? I could not get the visions, smells, touch, sounds out of my mind and body, which is exactly where they originated. I had been taken prisoner by my own ghastly fantasies.

However, in my incarceration I gradually became aware that there was a small window to the normal outside world. I was not completely deprived of the light of reason. There were just enough short periods when I would glimpse the sky from my cell, so to speak, and mercifully it did not fall down on me, as I so often imagined it literally would. Occasionally I even ventured out and found that I could converse quite coherently with another person. So there was still some part of me I recognised which could function with the material world.

But contact was threatening. I could not talk to others of my parallel existence. Although my stricken face sometimes betrayed me, my eyes being full of my ordeal with sockets hollowed through lack of sleep, I was always on my mettle. I had to be so vigilant. Any moment in my day or night when my mind was not totally engaged in the concrete 'here and now', it could be swept up into a whirlwind like rubbish in a yard. All the time I was scared of being seized by anyone or anything, that I would be taken back into my prison and have another full-blown psychotic experience.

Staying on this edge of madness was exhausting, and exhaustion left me even more susceptible to being overwhelmed. If I relaxed my guard then the hallucinations flooded in. My persecutory visitors however, were tireless. There was no let up at the end of the day either, when night fell. It seemed that darkness colluded in further barricading me in with these awful entities, while the fanglike shadows cast by any artificial light would play catch with me. I was easy quarry. Rest brought no respite. My eyes might close. But I could not shut off the malignant forces that were within and without. Indeed, for nine months or more while in the deepest throes of this breakdown, I survived each day on a maximum of two hours sleep. Moreover, these were full of nightmares and when I woke up I wished I had not. There was no refuge.

Most of the time, the outside world seemed to conspire with my inner world, the agreed plot being to finish me off for good. Paranoia ran rife. Yet still my predators allowed me to go on living.

But in one particularly devastating week, the real nature of death occupied me. My much loved German Shepherd dog had been deteriorating in health for many months. As mad elements ganged up and gathered strength around me, I begged her to stay by my side for a little longer – she who slept outside my bedroom door each night, my loyal friend with her deep, soft eyes - always there for me. But it was not to be. So I held her close as we shared our last hours together. Her name was Amiga and she was a true soul mate. Now I was without her and life felt even more unsafe and desolate.

However I was left with my budgie who sustained me for while. But then he died and I was completely alone again, apart from my unwelcome visitations which came cheek by jowl. So I bought a black kitten I named Isis after the goddess of the moon - but coincidentally, she stayed for only a lunar year. The day before she disappeared, I had a horrible dream of her dying from starvation. Perhaps I did not have enough love to give her at this time. Was I doomed to lose all that was stable?

Another period without any house mates ensued, until I took in a couple of cats. These two would snuggle up with me on the rug I wrapped myself in each evening. Cats are naturally selfish creatures and whatever comfort I drew from them at this time of great need, they survived. Moreover, the three of us have maintained over the years a mutually affectionate and satisfying attachment; a relationship which does not compromise the need to follow our instincts and lead separate lives. I like that. Cats are ideal, if somewhat extreme, models of *individuation*.

So I received just enough sustenance from these fellow creatures to keep me going and, despite all that befell me throughout this crazy period, somehow, I managed to feed my pets and maintain contact with a few close people. I feebly clung to these straws and gleaned an existence.

But, for the most part I did not know whether I was coming or going. Now I wonder how I did manage to keep body and soul together, as negotiating basic everyday tasks took an inordinate amount of effort. Moreover, any excursion into the outside world for essential provisions brought me out in a cold sweat and I would have a major *panic attack*. It felt like the mayhem which reigned within me was out there in the streets and marketplace.

I must have been a liability to myself and others when travelling away from home. However, in my mind, in the capsule of my car I was less exposed to danger than on foot. I had a steering wheel to hold onto which gave me some purchase. The vehicle's body seemed to contain me. It provided an edge against which I could measure myself and thereby check out and find some direction. While getting my 'head into gear' was difficult, the mechanics of operating my car seemed simple enough to make me feel that I was in charge. But I was not really safe on the road.

However, when forced to take a trip on the London Underground, which I tried to avoid at all costs, then the idioms 'stuck in the tunnel of time', 'down the tube' and 'strap hanging' became a concrete reality for me. Rather than seeing myself standing alongside the ranks of fellow commuters who daily had to tolerate this conveyor belt mode of subterranean travel, I would experience myself as a piece of meat swinging on a hook with my life blood going down the drain.

On one such journey, I left the train three times, so desperate was I to escape the foul dread I was drenched by. But I did not realise what I had done until I found myself on a strange street outside some station – who knows where, I did not. Travelling on what is sometimes called the 'nervous system of London' is the pits at the best of times. But when you feel as if you are only just holding on, that your life is on the line, then it is the very worst of times. Being cooped up, like rats in a sewer, drives many people to behave oddly. It totally freaked me out.

Fear makes us flee, freeze, or fight. I did all three. Sometimes I tried to get away from the demonic forces – but to no avail. So I braced myself against their onslaught for a while. But I could not resist them indefinitely, so then I would collapse and be taken over. I was under siege and petrified. I seemed fastened to the spot – the nails once palpably being hammered through my feet.

Fear is a great inventor, a self perpetuating generator of the imagination which is infectious. My fear had no bounds. Fear creeps up on you from behind the screen of reasonable doubt. But when given the unrestricted space of psychosis to operate in, it can destroy its host. When psychotic episodes came thick and fast it was a dreadful time for me. Falling in and then crawling out of madness meant that I had terror in the psychotic experience, and also, the terror of returning to that place, maybe for ever.

Thus I can well understand how some succumb to psychosis, rather than stay on this horrifying seesaw existence. What I needed was a point of balance. What I found, when I reached out for help, was that most people tipped me one way then another, ever closer to the madhouse.

Should you find yourself becoming caught up in this terrifying world of mine and groping around for a guide rope to steady yourself, here is one, albeit difficult to grasp as it has a twist to it. What I discovered, in fits and starts, was that the fear of going totally mad began to initiate creative action in me.

But many signals passed me by. Finding a lasting way out of my crazy arena was very erratic, not straight forward at all. Looking back then ahead and more importantly to the present, I came to see – and this is another paradox – how I actually needed to welcome in these formidable manifestations. Although seemingly trying to exterminate me, they were, in fact, trying to prod me into seeing different aspects of my self – undercover agents of my psyche which might come on side and work for me, perhaps.

Something had to give if I was not to remain powerless, locked in terror with my psychotic elements and cut off from consensual reality. Yet it seemed more vital that I resist. Surely if I were to tender myself, I might give in completely – anything to escape the intolerable pain of becoming fully conscious. Indeed, without my stalwart therapist and my own knowledge of the psyche to provide a frame of reference, I am convinced that I would have become a long-term inmate in a psychiatric institution. But while I escaped such enforced restraint from external authority, for a long time I found myself fettered by my own crazy spectres – only too often played out for real.

The more I strained against them, the tighter their hold on me. And that is how I eventually realised that I had to replace these hallucinogenic shackles with some mental and physical boundaries of my own.

Madness is all the paradoxes you can imagine rolled into one. Enlightened freedom embraces contradiction.

On the one hand I must accommodate my psychotic entities. At the same time, I needed to convert the *delusion* of aggressive forces surrounding me into real, effectively assertive boundaries. This basic energy needed to be utilised. In symbolic terms, I had to round up the escaping wild forces without culling them. I must bring them into a higher level of consciousness, so that they were under my control. Yes, the principle of transformation was promising. But might I be the one to lose my head in its execution.

Ultimately what freed me was a resolute commitment to my therapy sessions. Here I was able to build for myself, little by little, a container adequate enough to hold the monumental forces which sought to possess me. That is why my professional work with others also tempered, and brought greater coherence and management of, this psychotic realm.

I was determined to continue working as this afforded a tenuous structure in my life and demanded the discipline of keeping to a strict code of ethics. It sounds implausible now but somehow, I managed to find a foothold on reality whenever I stepped over the threshold of the clinic of complementary medicine where I practiced.

Maintaining this responsible role was a relief. It also

brought additional pressures. Taking these short breaks back to work out of madness, helped me to refocus. It also deepened my recognition of the disorder around me. I found that I could contain my psychotic elements from running riot in me while in my professional role. However, they still lay near the surface. The crazy imaginings that were so alive to me could fire up my clients' deepest pathological issues. All sorts of bugs came scurrying out of the woodwork at this time - theirs and mine.

My work was under constant supervision. I had to monitor myself closely and listen to others' recommendations as to whether it was in my best interest, and that of my clients, for me to continue to practice. Naturally, there had always been some mutual contamination between clients and myself. But now I was more in touch with what had been lurking in my deep unconscious. It seemed like open season for all comers.

It was a question of assessing whether I could *integrate* this material sufficiently so that I might support my clients in managing similar elements in themselves. I remember how a self confessed *sado-masochist* sought my help. Previously I had not realised how open I was to attracting this particular dynamic. But along with my flood of consciousness came vital recognition of how, in order to function responsibly, it was essential that I protect myself and my clients. I referred this client elsewhere.

This chapter ends with the beginning of my madness. So far I have gone back and forth from my crazy depths to some form of survival tactics, without referring to how I came to be in this state.

A few, like Jung (1963), have consciously chosen to visit the psychotic realm and found, with patient work, that the door back to sanity was not slammed shut behind them. In some way I also made the decision to descend into this nether world, although at the time, little did I know what I had let myself in for. I wanted to escape, run from what I did not want to recollect of a horrifying time in my childhood but which was, nevertheless, coming up from my deep unconscious. However I was struck by a powerful image which compelled me to face what was before me.

In my mind I saw a sprite, a harbinger of the devil, standing at the top of a ladder which was leading to the door of hell's inferno. Entwined through the ladder was a snake. As a child, the board game of snakes and ladders had always enthralled me. What was surfacing from my unconscious seemed irresistible and irrevocable.

Was I mistaken? Have I lost more than I gained? Am I *reframing* a mental breakdown into a lucky break? As I cannot go back to how I was, am I turning a negative into a positive to reassure myself that it has all been worthwhile? I do not think so. For having stepped through the gates of madness, eventually I was to re-emerge with a most precious possession - my self.

The summary to the question of madness is a bit of a riddle so that you might come up with your own version, as it lies in your answer to, 'Who am I?' If you think you are going mad, there is hope that you might find it a healing process. On the other hand, if you have never been in touch with madness you might be missing an essential part of you. If you protest that you are sane and the rest of the world is mad, you might be right or, perhaps, it could be the other way round.

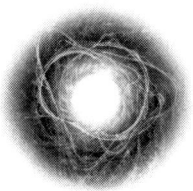

Chapter 2

An Energy Beyond The Boundaries Of The Body

I am a porous vessel afloat on sensation, a sensitive plate exposed to invisible rays ... tacking this way and that through daily life as I yield to them.   Woolf, 1994

*M*y account of how madness transpired continues but now moves into a critical period when I began to accept that what seemingly beset me did, in fact, belong to me. In theory this meant progress. But these powers were so much stronger than rational thought. Acceptance was easily turned into submission.

Thus, after months of experiencing unremitting assaults, dispassionately called hallucinations, it was a relief when my therapist nudged me out of being a passive victim. Knowing that my assassins would come again in some form or another, he suggested that I prepare for such invasion by surrounding myself with candles. This person rarely gave a directive or offered a definitive solution, preferring to trust in the therapeutic process. But I was fast becoming resigned to my mad turns and only an injection from another could summon enough will for me to take decisive action. 'In setting up a ritual, even as simple as this', he continued, 'you're taking some control.'

That night I made what felt like a pact with the devil. OK – so be it. This time I would be ready. With each candle I set up and lit, I drew a degree of strength. Thus I saw the candles growing into sentinels, their flames linked up into a chain of protection. With my eyes fixed on this ring of light, I waited.

Suddenly my body contorted as I became a skeleton manacled to a dungeon wall with only gnawing pain to convince me that I was still living. I was as cold as the wall of stones that interred me, which I counted like friends, and as foul as the fetid air which filled this hellhole. Rags of despair hung from my bones. I had been left to rot – of that I was convinced.

But was that smoke I could smell? I started to choke. First my lungs, then my flesh felt such burning heat. Painfully, I lifted my head and saw flames licking around me. The flames from the candles had manifested into a blazing pyre and it was my body, my mind that was melting in its midst.

Madness is totally nerve racking. It is alarming enough when, for the first time, we realise that we have been through a full scale psychotic experience. However the experience itself, in the moment, is an incredible blow to the human frame. As our mind disperses into fragments, all sense of orientation to what we once had an effect on is lost, seemingly for ever. Pandemonium breaks loose. With every subsequent hallucination comes a discharge of violent energies, impacting us with yet more formidable shocks.

Even small everyday events can be blown out of all proportion. It is as if we are constantly being bombarded from within and without. The body and mind are ravaged. Our whole organisational system of perception becomes overloaded as little is processed.

This is so, whether psychosis takes a beatific or demonic shape. In an idealising delusion or hallucination, we can feel embraced by divine love. Yet sadly, all we do is lose our self in such impressions. For such an expansive experience to inspire us in our personal life, we must already be connected to and be able to draw on a solid sense of self. Creative forces are synonymous with destructive impulses when there is no holding *psychic* device to integrate them.

Whether sublime or hostile, my experiences left my body in a constant state of gross hyper excitation. Its tissues were inflamed by the tingling energies shooting along its neural pathways. My usual reaction to such batterings was to be struck dumb and go into involuntary spasms. Rarely would I shriek in pain. I was alone in this and so what was the use.

But on this night when I felt I was being burnt alive, I cried out for help. Suddenly, I saw an angelic figure coming out of the fire. Its intense energy hit me so strongly that I gasped and immediately, felt flung out into the universe. I truly felt I was whirling in the stratosphere. And then I was left there, suspended in the vast stillness, surrounded by incandescent light, the radiance of which filled my body to the point of it singing. I wondered at the colours and force surrounding the globe. Mostly I remember the silence, how it seemed to hum in my ears such was its power.

Then, all at once, I was back with the glowing candles in my bedroom and I heard the words, 'It is done'. Gradually, very dimly I realised this 'death' was different. For the first time in over three months I had a moment of rest and a sense of completion. My circle of candles had contained me, enough for me to let go of some of my paralysing terror.

When I was hallucinating, all voluntary thought and action ceased, leaving my senses only keener. My body still remembers the sight and sensations of being ripped apart by a wild animal. It was black as a panther and it sprang out of the dark room. It had eyes like rapiers and teeth the size of a sabre toothed tiger. I smelt its hot breath, heard its snarl, felt savage claws raking my skin, teeth tearing into my flesh and its weighty impact on my chest as this ferocious creature lunged at me. It felt too much to bear, but I did.

The initial charge from most attacks hit through my feet so that my legs would jack-knife with my torso. My infernal beings revelled in the element of surprise. But one night I was struck from above. I watched in horror and felt the force of an axe as it came down and split my skull right through the middle - a somewhat macabre creation of a split psyche.

Some manifestations came so fast and with such fury; others came in agonising slow motion like when I felt laid out on an icy slab. Then I was stiff with cold and I shivered for hours afterwards. Another time, when seemingly pinned over a seething hotbed of coals, my blood felt at boiling point and when the hallucination passed, I was left with a fever.

All the time I was on tenterhooks and sometimes this was graphically played out. The first sign was when I felt my bed shuddering. Then just as time in tortuous strands, every sinew in my body gradually seemed to be stretched out and rent as my bed became a rack on which I was being dismembered. It was hard to assemble myself again, especially when my muscles felt so sore and bruised as a result. Another occasion, I felt a metal band being tightened around my neck, little by little, so my airways were being slowly cut off. I came out of that frantically gulping in air as if this day was my last - but it was not. My imagination was ace at crafting such torments and whether in the guise of instrument, man or beast, all felt real and left me utterly spent.

Back to the night when momentarily I was released from my shackles and the powerful energies manifested as the pure element of fire. The heat was on, turned up so directly that I was consumed in the flames. Was I giving up by giving in? Surely, in surrendering to the flames, I had allowed in these malevolent forces.

Wild as it might seem, in submitting to this terrifying ordeal, I felt a minute shred of will and sense of self had been reclaimed. Instead of trying to keep these psychotic elements at bay, I was coming to realise how they could 'in-form' me. They were, after all, a materialisation of my unconscious and a reconstitution of disorganised memories and corresponding emotions. They might have been very disparate fragments but combined into such powerful configurations, they demanded my attention. These forces delivered me to this state and so could get me out of it. Either I must take control and assemble them into some kind of order or they would take me over. The theory was coming to life.

Of course, at the moment of impact, there was no meaning; whereas now I can translate this particular night's psychotic illusion in terms of its essential elements. I see how the candles bearing the flame of love, and power represented by the fire set to extinguish me, had united and transformed into light. This then personified into the shimmering angel and expanded so fast that I took flight into the firmament.

I craved deliverance. The lighted candles had brought a flicker of hope. But in just registering this, it eluded my grasp. It was a trip too swift and forceful for me to integrate fully at the time or in the months thereafter. Out of the embers, my body needed to slowly consolidate into a stable structure. In the immediate moment however, these ashes had wafted away in the element of air - my mind - which was so diminished it could not contain them.

Is it possible to convey what is way beyond the realms of another's experience?

Should you find that your brain is being catapulted around the room or you are shutting down as you read about my mad episodes, let me say that this is not just a cathartic exercise for me. As the book progresses, greater meaning will unfold. More theory and logical thought will be included shortly. However, these graphic descriptions may impress on you the strength of a psyche's raw power and the 'pros' and 'cons' – yes they will emerge – in disrupting its structures. The case of the reactive unconscious which is psychosis will be unpacked with care, so that you might begin to understand how enlightened reasoning can come out of the chaos of madness.

If, in the meantime, you find a passage particularly difficult to take in, I suggest that you think on why the material feels such tough going. Put the book down for a while, rather than skip any pages. Better to take the matter of madness in small doses. Some accounts may press highly sensitive buttons which evoke a range of emotions such as fear, pain, boredom, incredulity, dissent, anger, shame, chaos, wonder ... there is no end to psychosis. Please feel your way carefully through the layers of madness as they reveal the intrinsic value of the dawning self.

I am not, however, recommending that you suffer, in reality, such prolonged and violent, extensive and alarming psychic attacks as I did. I went far beyond what it takes to journey towards self fulfillment and I know now where and why I went seriously wrong. I will come to this point in due course and, in turn, I will endeavour to show where parameters and safeguards lie.

When planning this book, in order to clarify the numerous feelings and ideas I had on the topic of madness, I drew a spidergram. The picture which emerged was of a somewhat frenzied spider who had lost a leg and so was going round in circles. ('Re-member' literally means to gather back, reconnect with what has been lost, severed.) My diagram showed so many lines of thought crisscrossing that it looked like this spider was also caught up in its own web. Such is the complexity and struggle in psychosis. Extracting simple threads of thought from memories of a jumbled mind, laced with highly charged psychotic matter, has been a challenging experience. I have a real love - hate relationship with documenting my soul journey.

While all creative ventures have their risks, there is quite a conundrum in this one. How can I describe what is so devastating to go through, yet still commend it as being a valuable experience? Glamorising or dumbing down such an intense psychic process would be grossly irresponsible. But suppose this reading material over stimulates your senses so you go beyond your comfortable emotional threshold. Will this effectively further alienate you from your own psychotic parts?

I hope that I have found the basis on which you might build enough trust to explore this sphere of the psyche with me. Since the subject we are addressing throughout is one of self exposition and self possession, for me to exhibit such openness seems paramount. In presenting the truth of my experience, my belief has grown that this could stir, sometimes resonate with, what lies deep within your being and you might have a heartfelt connection with this material.

Genuine sureness of self comes through knowing uncertainty. So it was for me, as I began to recount my tale, confused thoughts and feelings started to unravel and stabilise when I no longer censored what was really true for me.

But when everything that had once seemed reasonably solid and dependable was falling about my ears, it was very different. Then, if on a rare occasion I tried to describe to another what had been happening to me, I would be thrown back into the clutches of imaginal bodies. As my normal outer covering and internal filtering systems had broken down, in my recall I would be hit once again by the same excessive stimuli. I did try to communicate and ground these manifestations by painting them. Certainly the canvas served its purpose as a container but it could not fully portray to another what was etched into every cell in my body.

Unless you have experienced the mighty force of a psychotic episode, it will be hard to imagine the effect of its implosion within the fragile structures of what we call a normal functioning human being. Hallucinations may be considered 'all in the mind' but in fact, you not only see these images but you can feel, smell, taste and hear them – and suffer the after-effects. It is not just the psychotic who have experienced this amazing phenomena. A few people who have undergone deep hypnosis will know how this can induce the corresponding sensations and tissue reactions. However, when hypnotised, these effects are more diffused, contained and controlled by the practitioner.

Now the memory of much in this period has faded in intensity, my body's sensory mechanisms no longer surge in the same way when I think about it. Moreover the blur which once stopped me recognising what was reality and what was my psyche playing tricks on me, is very different from the filter which currently protects me from what was so awful to record back then. Time and laborious conversion of this energy has meant there is less fusion and a more refined route for processing my visceral responses.

Yet in the main, I have held back from speaking about my crazy world - not so much for fear of the emotional and physical effect on me and of being shunned but, because it was so bizarre and complex. Without explaining the whole experience, including the creative aspect of psychosis, as my writing allows, how could anyone comprehend it?

After my flights into insanity had subsided, I visited The Planetarium in London. Here, lasers and space photography were used to create in the audience the sensation of being propelled into the night sky. However as I sat there, I was struck by how my hallucinatory spin off the face of the earth felt far more vivid and authentic than what these special effects were producing in me.

In an art gallery, we might become very absorbed by a picture, and particularly perturbed if by the surrealist Dali. However there is always some part of us which remains in contact with our surroundings.

The same is so at a cinema when watching a horror movie. Despite the clever technical tricks which bring the audience into the experience of horror, the screen acts as a filter to the full sensation. Comforting reality is close at hand. We remain supported by our seat, there is a reassuring soul alongside and a familiar rustling of crisp packets nearby. We know that we freely chose to pay for this experience, we can walk out and that the show will end.

However, in the psychotic dimension there is no curtain and the backdrop, our mental frame, is so shattered that we are unable to organise what tumbles out from behind the scenes. There is no one in charge. All the sensations come at once so that the world speeds up or they consolidate completely and it comes to a grinding halt.

Of course, we all fluctuate in our moods. But our perceptions are extraordinarily exaggerated in psychosis. What is abstract becomes concrete and vice versa. But in this fluidity and fixation, nothing seems to evolve into anything that is truly meaningful. The shape and rhythm of life goes haywire. I tried to sort it out. But it was beyond me.

'Don't you just love flying. I often visit my friends this way.' Anyone overhearing our conversation would probably imagine that we were two jet-setting socialites or both high on *LSD*. In fact this comment was made during a sincere discussion on the sensation of self propulsion.

My companion was an inflated *narcissist*, a Peter Pan Barrie's (1988) fairy tale figure of eternal youth look-alike, who was prone to navel and mirror gazing, and flights of fancy. In the latter he was not alone, as I must confess to feeling pretty omnipotent myself when experiencing this flying phenomenon. I would see friends and family down below, mere earthbound mortals, viewing me with such awe which only served to fan my already expanded boundaries, thus I spiralled ever higher.

What I remember so vividly, was my certainty that I could really fly in my daily life. Flying was easy – if you thought you could, you did. Effortlessly gliding and surfing the wind currents you find there is no limit, not even the sky. I did not need Peter Pan to show me how. Sometimes, I would walk through walls. At the time I felt totally lucid. It did not seem odd, rather what was surprising was that I was not using these talents more often.

But then - maybe the phenomenon is not as crazy as it sounds. After all, science shows matter as particles of energy with a surrounding *force-field*. These normally invisible transmissions can be cast as spooky or New Age. But their perception was fundamental to primitive man in the 'dark ages', while the mystic, spiritual healer and Eastern medical practitioner has always worked with this matrix of energy.

And now a few scientists in the Western world who work with quantum energy are catching up with them. Soon the energetic field beyond the dense, physical mass, the etheric or subtle body in esoteric terms, might not be considered so strange or scary. Bio-electrical charges which stream through the human body have been seen to correspond to emotional changes and there is growing evidence that these particles of energy, expand in excitement and condense in depression. Maybe my dense, physical body was so excited that it was releasing its invisible, energetic body which was indeed moving through walls and flying.

Be that as it may, these metaphysical excursions not only felt totally real in the moment but I was unable to bring myself back properly into a physical reality for a long time afterwards. Herein lies the difference between night or day dreams and a psychotic experience.

You might have woken in the middle of a nightmare horror stricken, and for a short time remained with the full experience, until your senses received sufficient messages from your real environment that this was just a bad dream. Our psyche loves to play when *defence mechanisms* are not in place. Thus if deprived of sleep we lose dream time when unconscious desires and dreads can be played out. Without this receptacle in which to sort, shape and pack away these impulses, eventually they can overflow and merge with present reality.

While a latent subconscious thought or feeling appearing in a dream spans many different levels of the psyche, like a virtual reality game generated by computer technology, in contrast the hallucination is formed out of a very deep primitive thrust which has no mental container.

Everything would change from minute to minute when I was on the brink of madness. One minute the sight of the sky would uplift me into what at that particular moment seemed the grand scheme of things. Then just as quickly I would feel myself being physically pulled into the sun and burnt up. I could extend into areas of my psyche that stretched to the limits of creation or contract into a *catatonic* state.

The world as I once knew it was spinning out of control. Those who inhabit a psychotic world have little sense of time and space. Both bamboozle us – here now, then gone in leaps to aeons past or future. My centre of gravity was so askew. I would ricochet from flying in the galaxy to being flung as a cadaver into a subterranean charnel house. One moment I remember walking supreme on a high wire over an abyss, the next I dropped, hanging with the wire round my neck as a noose, a black bag over my head. Quickly recorded - but these events shook me and stayed with me.

However, I did have brief interludes in between psychotic performances which afforded a smidgeon of objectivity and balance. Similarly here, before considering more concepts of how we seemingly go beyond the boundaries of our body, the following might form a bridge back to the concrete mind, as it was for me when I could fix on the practical.

Sometime in the day or night I was able to carry out simple everyday tasks, and eat – a little can go a long way when self preservation is pared down to the essentials. Keeping tabs on what was happening in TV 'soaps' afforded a much needed break and some continuity. Even hearing about real major catastrophes in the wider world and heartbreaking stories closer to home, although exacerbating my stress, reminded me that there were others out there whose lives were also in disarray. It was consoling to know I was not the only tormented soul.

Sometimes I would watch the sun set from my living room window, and when it did not drag me down into its fiery chamber, I would enjoy a glass of wine. In this I risked becoming even more 'out of it', but when I initiated a distraction, even a hazardous one, I was in charge. It did not just happen to me.

Thus terror loosened its stranglehold occasionally and I began to be gentler with myself so that the idea of setting aside a particular day for the sole intention of staying 'in the moment' took hold instead. It was a one off but what a day it was. A day when I could recoup my energy, attend to my heart and follow my instinct. I noticed and embraced with wonder every detail of what I encountered. Whether it was in the fairy tale I read, a flower or puddle in my garden, I found that I could delight in whatever caught my attention. Moreover, to my amazement, I realised that I was breathing more freely.

But mostly, I felt the violent impulses running through, and streaming out like frayed ribbons from my body. I was attuned to agony, rather than peace. Sleep disturbance further took its toll. My worn-out form had little time to 're-cover'. Either I was caught in an immobilisation of energy and totally cut off from my body and surroundings, or I felt disturbed by the slightest of stimuli. The smallest and simplest of things seemed to hold extreme significance or none at all. I would view the world through the alert eyes of a frightened child or with the tired eyes of one who has seen too much. Overall however, I perceived that life held little purpose, love or beauty.

How many of us have not at sometime driven a car while a part of us is 'away with the fairies'? Most of me, however, was in a parallel, past or future universe. It was a multi-dimensional convergence that felt very real at the time.

'*Chi* energy goes walk about at four o'clock in the

morning', explained the Chinese professor of Oriental medicine whose advice I had sought, 'which is why so many people die at this time.' In *flashbacks* to my childhood, when some violation of my body became unbearable, I would witness the scene from above. My body, mind and emotions may have been ravaged by the abuse but some essential part of me remained at a relatively safe distance. And over many months following these memories, I could be suddenly flung back to this suspended state and feel the danger of reclaiming my body - a horrendous experience.

When someone disembodies, a thin stream of energy maintains a connection between body and soul, so psychics and some scientists believe. This connecting thread I liken to an umbilical cord. In utero and early infancy, we remain merged with mother and open to source as many of our filtering systems are unformed. In a disembodied state, we feel similarly at one with another dimension.

Have I really been off the face of the earth? Or, was I just out of my head, perhaps in the three quarters of the *cortex* brain normally not utilised. Or, was genetic material stored from the beginning of time when fish flew and the gods were seen to walk the earth, flooding up from my *reptilian* brain.

Hallucinations hold both natural and supernatural forces. They span and mix elements from the *personal unconscious* and also the mythological or divine *collective unconscious* (the psychic area pooled by all). So much of my psychotic experience seemed to have an archaic tone, as if I had stepped into an earlier time, perhaps a past life. Occasionally they seemed to arise from what was still to come. None however seemed strange in the moment, nor in the few days which immediately followed the experience. The situations felt familiar to me - they still do to some extent.

It might be sensible at this point for us too to come back to earth, so to speak, and to explore these far reaching realms from a more pragmatic framework. We now have the technology to take photographic prints of our physical force-field. From such observation a theory proffered is that an energetic shape can move out from the physical body. I know this. I also know of the weird sense of an attachment to my body below coming from my base *chakra*.

This phenomenon is an exciting, controversial area of exploration which falls into the domain of many different disciplines - theology, physics and medicine with their many branches including psychology, biophysics, complementary and fringe paranormal practices. As psychology holds a map which brings the ephemeral, other worldly, altered states of consciousness closer to home, we will consider this particular system briefly.

Moving down the out-of-body continuum, we come to the condition called *depersonalisation*. Common expressions used when we are mentally over stretched are of feeling 'beside ourselves' or that, 'we can't catch up with ourselves'. When in the twilight zone before we are properly asleep, it may feel like we 'awoke with a start' as if we had 'jumped back into ourselves'.

However in clinical depersonalisation, these feelings of being outside ourselves become our physical reality. So much so, we might not be able to see our face in the mirror. Scary stuff. 'Is anyone at home, anyone in there?' we might well ask when this happens.

A client of mine had little sense of her existence unless there was another person in the room with whom she could feel connected. She could not be with her self, when by herself. In a session, if words did not fill the space between us, she felt she was not there. Her psyche would go back and forth trying to find something to latch onto until it eventually spun into a vortex. She lost touch with her body.

Continuing on from depersonalisation is the state of *dissociation* when '*a group of mental processes is split off from the mainstream of consciousness*' (The American Psychiatric Association, 1994). This survival tactic allows us to escape to a safe place when the mind cannot manage intense emotional effects. To some degree, one section of the mind is detached from what another section is experiencing. However, if embedded as a patterned form of behaviour, different parts of a person split off so that each part operates as a separate identity. This condition, once known as multiple personality disorder, is called *dissociative identity disorder* according to the *Diagnostic and Statistical Manual of Mental Disorders (DSM 1V)* (Ibid).

I was never sure what identity one client would arrive in. Each had her own clothes and distinct ways of being. Realisation of this split came as a shock to her and making links to these different aspects of herself was a long, challenging but immensely rewarding process.

*

Hands up anyone who has not found their attention wandering when at a lecture. Being distracted is a common occurrence and generally we can come back to our senses and gather our wits quite easily.

However if such lapses in concentration on the present continue, we can end up with only the sketchiest of links to external reality. Then thoughts and emotions which belong in the past or future can run away with us and take us somewhere else. Some of us are so wound up that we can spend most of our lives cut off from the 'here and now'. We are all over the place.

It is all a question of boundaries. How often I have been reminded of this. Indeed, all such phenomena of feeling 'elsewhere' come when our physical and psychic boundaries are open and some contact is lost with the experience of our self in the immediate environment. Of course, this altered state of consciousness might be familiar, constructive and even pleasurable. However when extremely dispossessed, reformulating a full psychic presence is a formidable challenge. We are so far gone.

When psychosis ruled, rather than experience my therapist comfortably sitting at arm's length, where both of us could coexist and communicate over common ground, I would wipe him out completely. I could look straight through him into my own nightmare world. He and the immediate surroundings would disappear all together. It was too confusing, too threatening to correlate the outer reality with my inner reality. I had to wall him off because I needed to hold onto something - however bizarre and dangerous my inner milieu might be. I had to separate the two dimensions, otherwise they merged and he became part of my delusion or hallucination.

For most of the session, I would be swallowed up in my psychotic turmoil. If my therapist's voice did penetrate my world, I made it fit into my crazy scenario. I was under attack and he was leading the field.

On the rare occasion when his true note registered with me, I found it startling. Where was I? He declared my inner world was much stronger than my outer world. It certainly seemed like that to me so was good to hear. But written here on this page, it sounds so simple that it should be equally easy to rectify. However, turning around psychosis, by definition a condition of psychic confusion, is a bit like stopping dizziness having spun out of control.

The only thing that changes the momentum is when all the expanding and whirling forces get sucked in then shrink, and crunch - you disappear with them. Like Alice free-falling down the rabbit hole, I felt there was no stopping it. Sometimes, my psyche would become so overcome by horrendous emotions that it would empty. All was a dense black hole. I had blanked out everything but was left in the horror of a nihilistic state - until a new cycle of gathering forces would engulf then crush me again.

Society decides, with the law and psychiatry executing this judgment, the point where normal behaviour becomes abnormal and antisocial. Currently, the body of public opinion is loosening its hold on what it takes to be an upstanding citizen. It is no longer de rigeur to a maintain a 'stiff upper lip', 'thick skin' and 'steely backbone'. Attitudes have radically changed with greater emotional adeptness and now popular role models are celebrated for being 'open' rather than 'closed off'.

Our thinking and feeling functions have similar characteristics to our physical arrangement and corrective procedures may be applied accordingly – so I will mix the two here. Where there is body rigidity, it can take a forceful manipulation to return a dislocated joint which is out of normal range. It follows that, if we contorted our shape in order to fit into our primary environment, equally extreme adjustments might be necessary to our psychic structure. We may have to move way beyond the familiar bounds of our psyche, in order to come into alignment with our true life form.

Although rigid structures tend to fall apart when first extended beyond their usual range, ultimately our mental and physical health can improve greatly through such exercise. Where someone is placed on the disembodiment continuum can be determined by the distance the person has travelled away from being conscious of the body-self's existence.

As man explores the vast, rarefied realms of metaphysics, the veil which keeps us grounded on earth is getting thinner. Conversely, perhaps this closer 'under-standing' of the far-out dimensions will bring a wider, firmer base on which those considered mad can stand.

Of those who seek enlightenment, many are attracted to the transpersonal realm as an end in itself. I too tried to transcend malevolence in this way, and I know many others who stay on this high track. Such people are sometimes called 'space cadets' and I met a prime example when bordering madness.

She spoke as if she was from, and still on, another planet. Perhaps her heart was in the right place but her musical voice and sentiments of love and light seemed to me as if they were coming through the dissembling ethers like the songs of the Sirens (Grant & Hazel, 1973). Emanating from her were energies which wreaked havoc with the world around. Yet she appeared harmless enough. Her face was radiating perfect peace, while she was driving everyone else crazy. Angry confusion followed in her wake, as she scattered her darker debris about her, while sailing aloft unscathed. This lover of all things spiritual kept people waiting, lost others' belongings and expected everyone to look after her. Sometimes she forgot people all together. Only those who continued to feed her sense of magnificence were important to her.

A case which hit the newspapers a few years ago, was about a girl who became transfixed by the wonders of the infinite realms. So sure was she that just inhaling and absorbing the chi energy from nature was sufficient to nourish her, she took no food and embraced the earth - which was how she was found after many days, prostrate and dead.

As in all matter, we humans are governed by the laws of nature. When we solely seek omniscience without the surety of our denser foundations, we risk 'burnout' of our pure volatile elements. Throughout life I had always been something of a dreamer, looking for paradise, until I flew in the face of evil and saw it as a reflection of my inner demons. Yet while the most destructive of elements may be revealed in psychosis, so might the finest. The ferment in the psychotic layer may induce and convert base and life-giving elements so that these are purified and rise up. Just as the phoenix transforms out of ashes, so in our ego immolation, we eventually may fly high into the cosmos in safety.

But oh my goodness, this is such a fine rendering which is so much easier said or dreamed about than put into practice. Having engaged at depth with these turbulent forces, there can be no certain outcome that we will return as a truer whole. But surely, in the brooding darkness of our unconscious, the parlous fire of love and power pushes to be found, so it may transform into light.

The next chapter continues in this vein but includes more psychological constructs which might bring firmer ground on which we can play with the shadows of our mind more safely and freely.

Chapter 3

A Spectrum of Light and Dark

I am not I
I am this one
Walking beside me whom I do not see.
Whom at times I manage to visit,
And at other times I forget.　　　　　　　　　Jiminez, 1973

Where there are angels there are devils close by, however hard we try to split the forces of darkness from those of light. The two go hand-in-hand in religious texts, legends, nursery rhymes, poems, metaphors, myths and fairy tales. All are rich in using universal symbols to illuminate how, in order to see the shadow we cast on the world, we must know the full spectrum of light and darkness. Such sources of wisdom travel well. They filter through psychic boundaries, influencing spheres in our mind where imagination flourishes. But while imagination normally hovers at the threshold of the unconscious, it captures us in psychosis. So through image making we might access this basic and sometimes, paradoxically highest strata of psychic functioning.

So why are certain of our elements left in the dark? Do they remain effective and what can happen when light is thrown on them? These questions are addressed shortly and then illustrated by my own tale of how evil and goodness came to a head on a visit to the Somerset town of Glastonbury.

But let us begin with a couple of fairy tales. Some years

ago, well before my dance with the devil in psychosis, I was visiting my godmother who was dying and we were reminiscing, as one does so often at this juncture. She spoke of her surprise at my repeated requests, as a youngster, to listen to a recording she had of *The Happy Prince* (Wilde, 1966). The story had touched my heart. But as a child, I did not know why.

In this tale, a rich prince commissions a golden embossed statue of himself to stand in the centre of his principality where very poor folk live. A common sparrow seeks shelter at its base and begins to stir empathy and love from this rigid caste. In time, this replica of the prince begins to see the suffering all around him. His eyes are opened and he encourages the sparrow to give the gems therein and his gold leaf covering to his needy subjects. He weeps. Time passes and the winter elements further take their toll so that the sparrow perishes and the statue no longer shines. The town council orders the melt down of the defaced prince. There amongst the molten embers lie the hearts of the prince and sparrow, now united and they rise into heaven.

This story portrays how the soul qualities of love and compassion have been redeemed through the insignificant drab sparrow, rather than the lauded great bird of paradise. These images from long ago still bring a tear to my eye.

Another meaningful tale for me is of Will-o'-the-Wisp who was a ghostly character, seemingly an ugly man shrouded by a cloak. He came out of the mist and by the light of his lantern, guided travellers lost in the dark away from the surrounding bogs. Once upon a time, I played the part of Will-o'-the-Wisp in my primary school play. How I hated being cast as that gruesome character. I wore my cloak in shame. What I was not told by my teachers, until the very last minute, was that the fairy tale ends, as so many do, with me throwing off my mantle to reveal the prince that indeed I was. Thus in the classroom and on stage, my reign of glory as the prince was short-lived. But it was to be many years before I realised the significance of this late recognition.

Such stories of transformation abound in which it is first necessary to journey into dark places. For it is only through recognising, owning and integrating those parts of our self which remain hidden in the dark that we blossom into the fullness of our being. Out of the shadows we come into the sunshine.

Peter Pan from Never-Never Land lost his shadow and wanted a new mother to help him find it, (see Kelley-Laine's (1997) psychological interpretation of this story). The light from Tinker Bell, Peter's fairy friend, Will-o'-the-Wisp's lantern and the heart of the sparrow, are all symbols of soul which can reveal the shadow of our form. The moon, as well as symbolising mother, also depicts this element. Thus on the dark side of the moon, beyond the benevolent face, lies an unlit world.

*

There can be much more to us than meets the eye. Very early in life, we learn which of our characteristics are greeted with a smiling face and which are unacceptable to our parents, teachers and society in general. Although born with the potential to realise the whole of our self, so much of who we could be never comes into full consciousness or fruition - even the emotionally mature actualise only a fraction of their potential being.

Those traits that do not fit the ideal image get pushed away and rarely thrive. We develop accordingly. These seemingly 'lost' elements are *repressed* in our unconscious and become what is called our *shadow*. Sometimes we are so frightened of our shadow that we cut off from it totally and would not recognise it if we saw it.

Thus the person we present to the world does not always tally with our true nature. The preferred and cultivated identity, is often called our *survivor personality* which is further associated with our *false self*. I prefer to name this assumed persona, the 'adapted self'. Why? Because, while we may lose touch with a lot of what in us is original and genuine, we retain some trace of our inherent nature, regardless of how little this is nurtured by our primary carer. This core of our *true self* may be described as intrinsic, essential, real, innate, authentic, who we are, our essence and a manifestation of soul. You can call it what you like. If you have experienced it, you will know what I mean.

If connected to our core self, we know that to lose its integrity would cause the greatest of suffering. It is in this spiritual imperative for survival that martyrs choose a physical death, even if torturous and with no promise of life ever after, rather than to forgo the truth of their soul.

Of course, when the core being is welcomed in early life, there is no need to cover it with falsity. But some of us learn to adapt who we truly are so well that we come to believe this is all we are. We might major in playing the hero of the hour, the rebel or the mediator. There again we could take on the role of responsible carer. Although admirable in one way, if this was a condition of getting attention or being accepted in childhood the chances are that, while our survivor persona feels satisfied, our real self is ignored - this is true self denial and neglect.

But it does not stop there. We could also ride roughshod over another's fragility because it reminds us of our own. Naturally, in trying to hide our reviled aspect, we overcompensate in the opposite trait. In the shadow of the bully is a cowering victim and victims can share their torment with others. We cannot have one without the other. Our 'control freak' could well hold the lid on our craziness, just as our 'know-it-all' belies our ignorance and our 'toughie' covers our vulnerability. Whatever quality we add to the list, whether deemed vice or virtue, each can be driven by shame and fear of its counterpart.

Many of us are drawn to idolise and support those individuals who are living out our unfulfilled 'positive' feelings and attributes, only to then delight in their downfall. Also galling to acknowledge, we are particularly intolerant of people with 'negative' characteristics disowned in ourselves. A notorious example is how Hitler attributed his ambition to take over the world to the Jewish race.

Have you ever noticed that traits which really bother you in other people, are often those you cannot stand in yourself? Other people tend to mirror what we fear, are ashamed of and reject. How does this happen?

What is inherent is always with us, albeit unrefined through lack of cultivation. Aspects for which we are unwilling to take responsibility remain as trapped life energy, while the energy we use to shroud and deny them incubates the very emotion we are trying to escape from. Behind the screen, this expands and sneaks out into the world through the back door. And since our shadow is deemed so awful and threatening to our survival, just as in childhood, we attract others, often unwittingly, to whom we can attach it. We then feel a legitimate right to retaliate against them. Somebody else acts it out for us. 'It's not me, it's you'.

Nobody ever told me any of this, at home or at school. I wonder how many others there are like me.

*

Parts of our self which are totally split off can lead to extreme psychological states. They are figments because they do not exist other than in our febrile mind. But without the light of reason in which to reveal themselves, these anarchic forces may break out and encircle us. Shadow elements take on a life of their own. Once externalised, they can manifest as foreign entities trying to get in to us. Some believe they succeed. Satan or the Redeemer liveth.

When psychic and body boundaries are extremely open, elements from the personal unconscious may appear outside and energies from the collective unconscious can seemingly move in. The idea of being filled with the Holy Ghost could be seen in this way. Correspondingly, the antagonistic darker forces might escape or take possession of a person in the same way. A person with schizophrenia might manifest both extremes. (The social construction of madness is explored in Chapter 6.)

No longer do the majority believe that the devil can enter us and that madness is caught like 'flu. But quantum science seems to be verging on the possibility that, operating at a frequency range just beyond the dense physical, there might well be free-floating, malevolent and beneficial energies coming from both discarnate and incarnate beings. Such astral projections, I perceive, more easily attach to a person emitting vibrations of a similar frequency - although the host is generally unaware that they are on a such a wavelength.

Let us play with some simplified notions of how we initiate a chain reaction – the immutable laws of affinity. Energy is shown to attract like energy. If enough energy collects together, it will form matter. Scientific reports can explain this attraction using the theory of energetic patterning and brain cell activity. But better still, we can access evidence of this subtle action in our own life.

'E-mot-ion' is moving energy. If we fear something enough, we can produce that which we fear most. We unconsciously attract what we seek to avoid. Yet through this process of attraction, we can become conscious of more of our self - lo and behold it is there. If we can recognise that what we fear and dislike in others might be rejected aspects of our self, we might uncover and reclaim our totality. Our shadow comes to light.

When my force-field was wide open, such energies came very directly and evidently in a solid form. It was no coincidence. In the midst of my madness just a couple of days after my dog died, a dear friend from childhood telephoned me and blurted out how terrified she was of her imminent death. Having stoically born much suffering, she sobbed her heart out. This outburst was too much for her husband. In his rage, fear and anguish, he shouted down the phone that he would come and kill me. And in my frame of mind, I believed he would.

This was enough for me to feel the blow. I fell to the floor, the paralysed victim. When I came to, I rushed to close my curtains. I rammed bolts home and pushed heavy furniture against the doors. Then I waited, quaking behind my makeshift barrier. Imagination and reality were shoulder to shoulder. The supercharged forces which closely surrounded me were attracting equally deadly hostile powers from elsewhere. I felt severely unprotected, shocked and bereft.

Around this time, I also had road vehicles slewing into me and strangers accosting me, for no apparent reason. Dogs would launch an attack from a hundred yards away. And after repeated charges, I came to believe their apologetic owners when they said that their pet's behaviour was totally out of character. It was my fault. Of course, my body language and *pheromones* betrayed the free-floating fear that gripped me at this time. But I doubt whether these were detectable from such a distance and when I was behind the wheel of a car. So what was it?

The reason for these synchronistic unprovoked assaults was beyond me, or so it seemed. Yet, since my nerve endings were so hypersensitive, my electromagnetic field was equally expanded which explained why even remote objects would impact me. Thus, as I was firing off very high voltage forces and transmitting so widely, maybe I was also able to ignite reactive sparks in others far afield. Here I rest my somewhat sketchy case, as I have found no other feasible explanation. If only this fascinating subject had been in my school curriculum. Instead, I can but refer you to other radical sources and those which offer more scientific explanations and evidence.

In *'The Science of Philip Pullman's "His Dark Materials"'* (Gribbin, 2003) many of these wondrous phenomena are made sense of. Sheldrake (2003) writes of scientists being on the edge of understanding how our minds can reach out beyond ourselves and he cites experiments with people and animals which prove the effect of telepathy. McFadden's (2001) theory is at the cutting edge of proving such things. The best selling novel, *The Celestine Prophecy* (Redfield, 1994), focuses on how seemingly random energies, people, objects and circumstances, are drawn together. The books by the scientist, Brennan (1988 & 1993), explore how the body and psyche can be harmed and healed through this dynamic field. Boadella (1979) ties in brain mechanisms with energy fields generated in mystical and psychotic states.

Biochemists, neuro-biologists and psychologists are now more willing to share their findings on the links between mind and body and it is hoped that this pool will widen to include psycho-spiritual specialists, quantum and astro physicists. Through such cooperative work, we might develop more empathic and broader supportive structures for the mentally disturbed, both at a *neurotic* and psychotic level.

But meantime we know enough. If we enter the dark recesses of our mind and hold our shadow elements in our consciousness without necessarily acting them out, we are not so likely to attract such energies from outside. Emotions consigned to the shadow disable and contaminate. The old saying is wrong - what we don't know can hurt us, very badly.

What we turn a blind eye to not only clouds our self image and how others view us but also distorts our perception and judgment of the world. However we might try and 'con' ourselves and others, we cannot escape from our shadow. What we disown and put behind us out of sight, still follows us.

✷

In a dark time, the eye begins to see,
I meet my shadow in the deepening shade Roethke, 1960

My pleasing appearance when younger may have gained attention, while my unacceptable self remained concealed, forgotten like a stranger; that is until the dark time when my shadow caught up with me. Over the years, forces of volcanic proportion had built up inside me and these explosive emotions made themselves known through what felt like a three-pronged attack.

A few years prior to my breakdown, I had split up from my husband and in the space which that afforded, I began to project (see *projection*) my unconscious emotions onto my therapist. The trouble with facing the reflection of my shadow was that it produced mounting tension and fear. Eventually, fear descended into terror and I was inundated with flashbacks to being violated by my grandfather when young. So began the psychic and physical jolts. Everything, it seemed, was in the open.

Reliving this early dark secret, along with some corroborative evidence, also forced me to acknowledge that my boundaries were severely breached at the start of life - their very foundations were shaky.

In view of this, some supposed mentors encouraged me to undergo a re-enactment along the lines of Grof's (1985) stages of birth - despite my expressing concern as I felt so agitated. The effect was to immediately trigger severe dissociation. After this everything got so much worse. The full-scale hallucinations took hold.

My anger had never seen the light of day, not so far as I had been aware. Yet it was surely there, boiling away beyond a shadow of doubt. Not being in touch with this warning and protective agent, as a child I could not say, 'No' to being violated. Neither as an adult could I use this tool to defend myself in my current life.

The early, ongoing invasions of my form were being played out in hallucinations, alongside flashbacks, and reflected in reality. Spectres out of my darkest shadow were coming to get me and to take me where they willed. All the emotions of shame, terror, rage and agony which accompanied the past abuse and the current incidents, were compounding. Shadowy elements, too horrible for me to contemplate willingly, were increasing their pressure to be realised. I was beginning to feel terrorised by everything and everybody but could not recognise my own destructive urges. I could not push such forces away or release them from within, so they were imploding.

*

These wild sensations, sometimes manifesting as armies of ants or writhing snakes inside me, have a pulsing drum beat which I eventually recognise as 'You are wicked, wicked' - and each 'wicked' is reinforced by another beat from the wooden spoon, my mother's rage on the end of it, so that smarting pain is crawling up my legs and into my pelvis as she chastens me.

There was a little girl
Who had a little curl
Right in the middle of her forehead.
When she was good
She was very, very good
And when she was bad
She was horrid.   Longfellow, H. W.

I was taunted by this ditty as a child. My mother was for ever fussing with my hair, trying to train my wavy locks into a roly poly curl which fell onto my forehead. So powerless was I, that I withdrew into being a 'good girl'. I had to split off from everything 'horrid'. But I knew this girl in the poem. It was me.

Since infancy, the powerful weapons of shame and fear had been used to extinguish all sense of my anger and hate. Therefore I *retroflected* these feelings back on myself. I never went through the 'terrible twos' as a toddler. Throwing temper tantrums were not part of my repertoire.

I am talking about the 1940s' here and I had a mother who would have given Freud much food for thought when forming his theories on sexuality; while Jung would have had a feast day if he had met her when he was writing on the vagaries of religion. In my mother's mind sex was sinful and dark, yet I was exposed to it, and religion harshly ruled that I imbue love and light.

This resulted in my libidinous sexuality, primed too early, becoming my trump but also my rogue card. Flaunting my cultivated, yet reproved of, sexuality brought such confusion. But in early puberty, I felt too excited by this energy and therefore too wicked to continue my religious leanings.

As the years passed, however, I had the growing sense that something was missing and I sought redemption of self through mystical and magical pursuits. This search reached its peak when marriage and motherhood failed to supply me with any true sense of who I was. Since my intuitive faculties were vital to survival in childhood and my boundaries were so open from continual invasion, I found that developing my psychic powers was easy. But little did I know that, in playing with these subtle energies, they could transmute into the demonic.

I would slip into other realms, tune into distant airways and streams of consciousness. I allowed myself to be possessed by etheric energies as then, I felt more powerful in other spheres. Channelling wisdom from spirit guides, soul rescue work, spiritual healing and portending future events were my forte. I was trying to exemplify the lightness of being, rather than be incarnate in a world where the essential life principle is that light and dark are interdependent. Thus I was bound to fall.

*

My journey in and out of madness flung me to and fro across the supposed divide of light and darkness and when visiting Glastonbury, which is purported to be the gateway to Heaven and Hades, I had a major crisis of this duality. After six months of being worn down by my psychotic forces, I had sought solace in a house of non-denominational retreat in Chalice Well which lies at the foot of Glastonbury Tor. I needed help, and while resting in a room designated for quiet reflection on the top floor, I felt a rush of energy surround me and all the sensations of being rocked in an angel's wings.

The power and bliss in this embrace were quite a shock to my raw and fragile form. But eventually I asked aloud, 'Why me?' – to which I heard the reply, 'Because you are here'. Overawed by this experience, I took some time to gather myself together before leaving the sanctuary. Slowly I came down from on high, taking each tread very carefully and there, at the foot of the stairs, lay a single, pure white feather. I was filled with wonder. Such materialisations or 'apports', psychic mediums believe, are gifts from the world of spirit.

However, my sceptic stepped in. Intrigued, I went round the house checking for open windows and any visiting birds. I found nothing. Then I sought out the housekeeper in case she had been plumping the cushions, using a feather duster or plucking a swan for supper. She had not and when, rather shamefacedly, I told her my tale, she simply replied, 'Well, this is the place of the archangel Michael.' This was news to me but somehow her words, like the angel's, seemed to suffice and my heart felt full of grace.

Later that day, I was sitting half way up the Tor on a log. My eyes were closed as the sun was shining on my face and I was basking in the glow which remained from the omnipresence of the angel. I was singing out to the world, 'It's OK to be me', as I was brimming over with the glory and beauty of life. I was at one with the mysterious, pulsating cosmic energy which interweaves every living thing. It seemed natural then, when I focused back on the grass at my feet, that there I saw a carpet of wild flowers identical to an image I had seen just prior to being held by the angel.

Wow! I had never visited Glastonbury before, nor did I know of its connections with the 'other worlds'. Suddenly, I was jolted out of my reverie. There in a hollow on the edge of my idyllic flowered carpet, was a dead sheep with its innards ripped out. How could I have missed such a horrible sight when I first climbed to this spot? Then, more of the gruesome world came to blot out my perfect landscape. A man with a rifle approached me, demanding whether I had seen the dog that savaged the sheep … that hit me. My time of bliss had been brutally taken away and without more ado, I scurried quicker than a jack rabbit back to the sanctuary.

✻

My longing for solace and healing in Glastonbury reminds me of the closing words of *De Profundis*; which Oscar Wilde (1973) wrote from his prison cell about suffering physical privations and the torments of soul.

> *Society, as we have constituted it, will have no place for me, has none to offer; but Nature, whose sweet rains fall on unjust and just alike, will have clefts in the rocks where I may hide, and secret valleys in whose silence I may weep undisturbed. She will hang the night with stars so that I may walk abroad in the darkness without stumbling, and send the wind over my footprints so that none may track me to my hurt; she will cleanse me in great waters, and with bitter herbs make me whole.*

My intense yearning to be soothed by Mother Nature's bouquet came eight months after my outbreak of psychosis when few things proved to have a moderating influence on me. Taking it easy was hard. So in hindsight, it is not surprising that I found a garland of nature could only be gained by gladiatorial combat. It was Easter and *archetypal* forces of death and resurrection surrounded me. Even the wind seemed intent on buffeting me around and the rain spat in my face.

Rather than nature proving to be a gentle force for healing, I was finding its elements further stimulated and amplified my troubled psyche. But perhaps, had it been hot summer, when a liberal mass of humanity draws the elemental forces to a head in the Glastonbury Music Festival, I might have been party to some spontaneous combustion.

Well, at that time, it felt like wonders would never cease. But later that year at the end of autumn, I did occasionally find a happy medium. I would snatch spells in my small, walled garden where I could breathe in the surrounding energy and feel relatively safe. Yet I was so wrapped up in my dark, unruly undergrowth that my garden flora and fauna ran wild for a few years without me caring or noticing. Lost in my pathology, I could not see how much mess had accumulated around me.

Thus it was a significant day in the following spring when I felt the urge to tidy up my garden patch. I cleared the paths and beds of weeds and overgrown shrubs, then scattered seeds of the flower Love-in-the-Mist. These have continued to bloom and spread their beauty each summer and I view them as a fitting tribute to how seemingly fragile, yet robust is our hold on earth. We need just enough sustenance for our seed to take root in the dark earth, so that our soul might flower in the light.

*

Here, having taken a break in my story by going forward into a safer time and place, we will now go back to Glastonbury. There must have been moments when nothing amazing happened, but the ordinary was obliterated from my mind by the extraordinary. I was in a perpetual state of shock. In this chaotic period of my life, what was normal was lurching from one drama to another. And certainly, in enchanted Glastonbury, the beatific rode in tandem with the horrific.

So it was par for the course that the day after my experience with the angel, the carpet of flowers and sheep's carcase, further events filled me with feelings of grace and horror. I was visiting Wells Cathedral nearby and feeling privileged to be spending time alone in its round chapter house while harmonic choral strains rose up from the cloisters below. Slowly, out of the ether, a gentle presence filled the room and I saw angels, seated in a circle around its perimeter. They were simply just there. It seemed very natural.

While I had been a dab hand at communing with lost souls and stars, until now angels had not been my scene. Perhaps as I had been walking with evil for some time, I needed this visitation from infinite pure beings to restore some sense of goodness around me. Whatever, I was so thankful. Their appearance brought me a still, inner strength and I felt as sound as the bell which then rang from the famous cathedral clock, reminding me it was time to leave. I felt blessed.

Now that my 'lower and higher' mental strata are more interrelated, I can take such an experience into my reality or see it as a significant image inspired by the 'god centre' in my brain. It does not seem to matter whether angels are fact or fiction - the feelings induced have the same soul-making quality.

After my trip to Wells, I returned to Glastonbury well nourished. I strode up to the top of the Tor and surveyed the stunning vista which encircled me. The setting sun spun spectrums of gold, purple, pink and blue and with wide open boundaries, I conjoined with the universe and felt the fulsome swelling of a *peak experience*.

But then the sky changed its mood. Once again, I was torn from my blissful altered state as thunder claps rent the air and with them came bellows from a man nearby, certainly deranged who, like my *alter ego*, cursed me, the world and everything in it. Dark rain clouds let loose their ammunition and wiped out the canopy of heavenly beauty which had enfolded me. So, as I had done the day before, I beat a hasty retreat to the house of the angel.

That evening, I came close to ending my life. I had had a lethal dose of morbid despair mixed with euphoria and this brought the impulse to kill myself. Elements which I once had split into divine beauty or base demonic, were in the same turgid boiling pot. I was a mess. My innards felt rent, my head pulped, all sanity seemed to have left and I spun into terrifying confusion. This madness was a fate worse than death. Death was preferable. The wherewithal to carry out the literal deed lay in my hands.

Taking one's life is considered to be a violent act against self and others, a way of demonstrating one's suffering, a cry for help, an extreme drive to escape purgatory and even an act of revenge. I just wanted to quietly leave behind the agony which engulfed me. It never crossed my mind as to how my death would affect my family, friends or clients. The pull to oblivion was mighty.

What stopped me? Daft as it may seem, it was the thought of how my unchaste body might desecrate that sacred place which prevented me from committing suicide. I heard my mother's voice. Her obsession with smelly bodies and keeping things 'nice' clicked in.

Following this programmed response came the nagging doubt that premature death was not a final solution anyway. I might return in a future life only to face this same awful predicament. There was nothing else for it but to take my bedding to the room where the archangel Michael had appeared, and there I passed a sleepless night huddled on the floor.

Now I knew well how the intensity of light and love is juxtaposed by the depth of darkness and hate. No longer could I sustain my sense of utopia on Glastonbury's hills and in the vale of Avalon which had reminded me of Eden. Almost fifty years after my birth, these opposing forces which I had never managed to truly own or balance had grown to huge proportions. They were battling away inside my frail form and being played out around me in the arena of Glastonbury.

*

Holding the tension of the many agents of light and dark is always difficult and therefore often they stay divided or eclipse each other. Our framework will be severely challenged if occluded forces, having been insulated in their 'savage' state for many years, clash with those in the light. It might seem impossible to bring about a ceasefire, let alone ongoing dialogue and conciliation between them. This deadly mix may well fling us into madness.

But using the notion of alchemy that base elements can be transformed into gold, so it follows that within a pot of psychotic ferment, there lies great treasure which might sustain us in life.

One of the many paradoxes about soul-making is that its reward is the most valuable and unique a person could have, and yet its raw material is often the most despised and common.   (Moore, 1992)

To bring our true light out of the darkness requires us to pare down to our most elementary substance. Exploration of source is vital. The root and remedy of psychological health and our soul's yearning for totality of being lies at the very beginning of life. In the next chapter therefore, let us delve into some basic, early developmental theory so that more light might be thrown onto the mass of emotional material accrued so far in this book.

*

Chapter 4

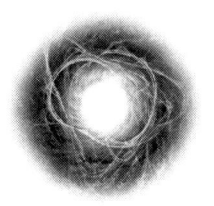

A Construct of Self

Section A

When I look I am seen, so I exist. Winnicott, 1971

Fortune shines if we fall in love with our self when young because life mirrors the way that we relate to ourselves. Ideally, as a child we learn that we are loved for who we are, and that we do not have to do anything to deserve and receive this love. Thereby we come to know that love is not to be acquired, earned or produced. It is just available. It is, unconditional (see *unconditional positive regard*.) Many parents aspire to this ideal model. Most are well-meaning people who believe that they are acting in their child's best interest.

This chapter examines various effects of child rearing, from the worst to the best. A particular focus is on how the *primal forces* are dealt with because, if basic needs, *drives* and emotions are not contained and mediated when young, these remain as potential psychotic material. Section A addresses infancy. Section B looks at the toddler stage and also at how shame and fear subjugate an emerging self and thereby lay the base of mental disorder. Since none of us are perfect human beings, to a greater or lesser extent, everyone has experienced some deprivation in childhood. Therefore, thoughts on re-parenting our self when adult are included in Section C.

A child's development is complex and there are many theories on the subject. Some people subscribe to the idea that parenthood comes naturally and that we should just follow our intuition. After all, motherhood is deemed to be a labour of love. It surely is, and if in contact with her own true, deepest nature, a mother will naturally appreciate and facilitate the originality of her offspring. Thus the relatively simple notions presented here are probably best appraised by reflecting on how you may have been affected as a child and how as an adult, others respond to psychological shifts within you.

What also needs to be taken into account is that a child's disposition can make connecting to his family difficult and vice versa. He may be genetically more wilful than loving, for a start. Also, his characteristics might not fit in with his particular home environment. For example, the sensitive, artistic child may remain a mystery, sometimes a feared intruder, to his down-to-earth, scientific or sporty family. Belonging to a family means two-way care and, while a youngster needs to be animated, he similarly needs to touch the hearts of other members.

Thus the onus of responsibility cannot be put one hundred percent on the primary carers, particularly when a child's base of experience expands into the wider world. However, while the majority of primary relationships are good enough, my proposal is that greater understanding of how babies and adults interact will benefit everyone.

Traditionally, the greatest influence on a baby is his mother as she is primarily responsible for his care, with father offering important support for both of them. Nowadays, however, modern man is more ready to take on the principal mothering role, as might a partner or another family member. Still, as the feminine qualities are of major importance in the first few years of life, in the text, I refer to generally the 'mother' but sometimes, to the 'parent' or 'primary carer' - and, for clarity, I use the masculine pronoun for the baby.

*

We like to think that there is an inherent bond between mother and infant and that through this connection the baby learns all about himself and others. Evidence indicates that a mother's attitude, even to her unborn child, helps to shape his sense of selfhood throughout his life. The first hour after birth has been found to be the perfect time for mother and baby to get to know each other through mutual gazing, smelling, listening, touching and tasting.

Yet for the newborn, reality is only what is within. People and things, therefore, are not experienced as 'outside'. Sensations have yet to crystallise into a core feeling of self. For the first few months an infant believes that he is the centre of the universe, assuming his mother to be part of him as in utero. Warmth and food is mother or whoever is the closest carer. This state is called primary *narcissism*.

For an experience of self existence to develop, a baby is totally dependent on, and vulnerable to, an autonomous 'other'. Just as 'we are what we eat', so a baby is made from the emotional feedback he absorbs from his carers. When being nursed, an infant will stare intently into the face of whoever holds him. Looking for what? Of course he is seeking reassurance and recognition of a familiar face, but also he is searching for affirmation of himself.

In infancy, we see ourselves as we are seen through the eyes of another. But if our mother figure is depressed, and therefore 'absent', we may only gaze into vacant eyes and feel lost, or rejected if they are disapproving, consumed if they are needy. She might reflect back an image of the person she wants us to be or fears we might be – someone who has both the 'positive and negative' traces of her own shadow, perhaps. We internalise the *mirror* of our self which is held up to us. Others construct us.

If only adults could more readily see the world through the eyes of an infant. It can be challenging to pause and consider how we may have felt when cuddled by our mother. Who and what might we have seen reflected, when we gazed into her eyes?

A baby is seen as cute, cuddly, innocent, helpless, an adorable bundle of joy and sometimes, a demanding monster. He can be all of these. However, so much can be projected onto this newborn soul that only certain characteristics are cultivated.

When our self expressions go unrecognised by our principal carer, we feel 'an'nihil'ated' – 'nihility' meaning nothingness. Not knowing or loving our true substance, deep inside we will feel empty. Having been cut off from our fundamental sensory and emotional self, it is as if we do not exist. We come close to a state of non being.

The most basic fear is separation from human contact and therefore no confirmation of self. The fundamental concern we all inherit is towards our source of comfort, protection and food - experiments with infant monkeys and dummy caretakers, show the preference in that order. Thus what threatens the supplier of our emotional and bodily care, threatens our survival.

As it happens, a baby intuitively knows his mother's needs. As long as he fulfills them, he has some measure of security and he readily absorbs her unconscious emotions. It is not uncommon for a mother to use her malleable baby as a receptacle in this way. In the extreme, the child is an object to be picked up, dropped, opened up or shut up according to her needs.

Although construed as love, a mother can be devoted to her offspring as a *narcissistic* means of self satisfaction. He is the 'apple of her eye' and she 'loves him to bits'. Her baby, however, is 'loved' for what he provides, rather than she be his source of a strong and stable self assurance. She seeks to alleviate her emptiness and longing to be the centre of attention, this never having been satisfied when young, through her baby's loving eyes.

Rather than he be starved of attention, he sacrifices his real needs and emotions, as an infant must preserve his primary carer at all costs.

*

So what is the difference between emotions and feelings? Emotions - meaning 'energy in motion' - are basic reactions. Feelings are judgments arising from connections we made in the early stages of our development between a response from another to our emotions.

For example, the skin of a newborn baby being bathed registers exposure and sudden temperature change which turn into alarm signals and so he may yell. If the mother disregards his emotional reaction, perhaps continuing to be cheery and playful, he might similarly associate bath time as nothing to be concerned about. Messages of alarm within his body might automatically become converted into a feeling of excitement. This may sound all well and good - bath times should be fun. But all sensory warnings need acknowledgment. (Chapter 5 Section B: 'Ongoing mind-body patterns' expands on such physiological processes.)

Alternatively, a mother panics at her baby's signs of alarm so that, to him, such bodily signals become associated with, and are felt as, a loss of control. There again, a mother might berate her baby for showing signs of fear, or laugh at him, so that he learns that alarm is confused with feelings of anger, rejection or ridicule.

Had the mother conveyed sufficient concern and appropriate reassurance towards her infant's emotional distress, if faced with a threatening situation in the future, he could similarly respond to his natural emotion of alarm. He may also feel excited, able to support himself and to take remedial action.

Infants can also have boundless trust and swim underwater without being alarmed. Thus primary carers need to clarify such perceptions, without passing on their own maladaptations, and demonstrate and initiate a response which their offspring follow. Thereby ways of keeping themselves safe are laid down.

However, rather than protect, a lot of unnecessary fear can belong to past conditioning. I know a man whose mother responded badly to his excitement when young and who, to this day, feels afraid of showing his excitement.

How we structure our world and coordinate or polarise fantasy from reality, in adulthood, depends on the attunement between our primary carers and ourselves in childhood. If what we tried to express about our inner experience was empathically mirrored back to us, then our primal forces will have turned into reasonably manageable, recognisable and *differentiated* feeling states.

✽

Mother is needed as a repository. When little, as well as trying to put our unprocessed material into our mother in order to convey what we are feeling, we also need this to be contained by her. We fear being overcome by such stimuli as hunger pangs or cold. They are too much for us to cope with on our own. So all we can do is cry out as a signal of what seems like our potential dissolution. Indeed, any discomfort may be felt as hostility inflicted on us.

Furthermore, our impulse to feed and take in love feels as if we are also consuming mother – especially when we find that we have teeth, metaphorical as well as physical, which can hurt. Not only do we absorb her life-giving elements lovingly, but also with a furious need. How can we sustain our mother when we need to feed off her, physically and emotionally? This challenging ambivalence comes to a head when we try to assert ourselves as a toddler – more on this later. However, as it is hard to know where we end and mother begins in the first few months of life, we feel particularly bad about this cauldron of energy.

What if our mother has not sufficiently integrated her own primal drives? Firstly, her skill and space to accommodate our forces will be limited. Generally, she will try to subdue those elements in us which she is not comfortable with, within herself. For us, these unacceptable emotions and urges will then become more treacherous. Secondly, while most of this control will go on at a subliminal level, we may well take on our mother's distress arising from our demands. Our forces can but conjoin with hers, and/or we feel wiped out. With no mental framework, no self regulation or adequate containing mother, we have nowhere to put this amalgamation of awfulness. This is madness in the making.

In this case, an infant might only turn the conflicting forces back on himself, retroflect them if he is to maintain the necessary fantasy of a loving connection with mother. In such a change of direction, hate and love can become so confused that one is indistinguishable from the other. Vital energy, sometimes called *libido*, is split off along with this undifferentiated material, and there is a void where the intrinsic self should flourish. Rather than develop a firm sense of what he feels, so a surety of who he is, he is always on edge, fearing annihilation.

∗

How could such a tiny bundle, who seems to epitomise innocence and frailty, harbour such raw 'animalistic' energies? I would not have been convinced of the fierceness and instability of the impulse-driven world of the infant, despite evidence from clinical trials, without coming to know this power for myself. You might ask, how, as an adult, I could feel what it is like to be an infant. Of course I can never be totally sure, as memory can play such tricks. However, I have *regressed* to moments which felt like and had all the hallmarks of infancy.

One experience was of feeling trapped in the birth canal, then of being forced out into the world and holding back what is called the 'primal scream'. On another occasion when I was extremely vulnerable, I whimpered like a newborn baby. But the most momentous and memorable experience was when it seemed like I was actually touching, smelling and seeing the milk-engorged breast. I remain amazed at how these natural primal sensations came with such a mighty upsurge that they flooded my whole being.

Imagination or recall? All I know is that incidents such as these equate with experimental studies that demonstrate how we arrive showing every intention of fully engaging with another. We start life with a great source of powerful urges and emotions which provide the potent thrust needed for living out our potential.

When in this primitive state, I longed for the bliss of soft substances, warmth, good smells or cooing soothing sounds. But there were more alarming urges. Once in a while I had a frantic impulse to bite and kick when I felt thwarted, particularly if by my therapist who I saw as both instigator and saviour of my distress.

Such was the diversity and rapid oscillation of these primal impulses heaving within, that I desperately wanted to vomit. I needed to empty myself of this seething mass which had been bottled up inside me - but a life long ability to stuff it down prevented such a graphic eruption. Of course, rather than 'spill my guts', this unprocessed material needed to slowly turn into 'food for thought'. But the sensations were so wild that there was no way they could be held onto long enough for sense to be made of them. Moreover, without any psychic organisation such urges could not transform into feeling states I could name and communicate in any meaningful language. So I swallowed hard and they became inert. I was struck dumb by the horror and went back towards vacancy. I had no words.

However, as time passed, ever so slowly and with great difficulty, I began to bring up what I could not assimilate when young. To begin with, sounds came out as drivel, swirling around in the empty space, and turned into blabbering nonsense. I was trying to form words but was talking 'double Dutch' like a garrulous baby. It was as if I was starting from scratch, learning for the first time how to speak as I endeavoured to construct and arrange thoughts around these primal urges. All this in order that someone out there might know how I felt inside.

※

Healthy primal attachment moderates and stimulates sensory and emotional arousal. If our mother responds to us as a baby by consistently holding and diffusing any inner turmoil, then, by many repetitions of such intervention, our trust in surviving these onslaughts grows. Through such cycles of collapse and then finding ourselves revived through another, gradually we are able to sustain the sense of ongoing 'beingness' - which is quite an achievement.

Realising just how difficult this delicate, complex and vital process is for mother and baby will, I suspect, depend on whether you draw on your experience and imagination, past and current, as you read about these developmental issues. Such self exploration is more precious by far than words. Therefore I would encourage you to linger a little along the way, in order that any free-floating thoughts and feelings can catch up with you.

The primitive instincts and emotions we are born with have to be reworked with our primary carer many times. These primal forces are the blueprint of who we are but need to be absorbed by our mother who then 'regurgitates' them back to us in a digestible form. Gradually through this refining mechanism, they can transform into our own unique feelings and thoughts, so we might make meaning of and express who we truly are. By this ongoing dyadic process, we come to recognise, accept and regulate our raw energy.

The mother, at ease with her own intense emotions, will see these as the building blocks of a true self, rather than as evidence of an unruly or sick mind. The infant's endeavours to express his primal forces will be similarly respected. Both can relax in essential developmental tasks including play, rest and in just 'being' together.

The feeling of security when an infant is physically and emotionally held in congruence with his particular needs, allows him to merge any sensations of anxiety he has with his carer's composure. This soothing holding cannot be faked. A baby will surely feel, at a sensory level, the difference between what is acceptance or sublimation and what is suppression. Yes, he is yelling because he is frustrated, frightened, lonely, over stimulated, bored or in pain. But it is OK, she knows, understands and is not too fazed by his outburst. How he feels - therefore who he is - is affirmed.

What is not always appreciated is that the distress of not being understood sufficiently can be more harmful and overwhelming than the sensation which the infant was originally feeling and trying to convey by crying. The silence of a sleeping baby which can follow mounting frantic cries does not always indicate that he is overtired. It might be that he has given up trying to get the right response from his mother.

If we reach the point of defensively closing down when over stimulated, especially when communication remains pre-verbal, then much damage has probably already been done. Being able to cut off from strong sensations, to repress extreme emotions and internal conflicts, might be considered a fail-safe procedure; it certainly saves our sanity in the moment when there is no one there to help relieve us. But using such short term survival methods might mean that our body becomes an incubator for madness.

Throughout life there will always be a shortfall between emotional trauma and our capacity to process it fully. Anyone who has ever tried to speak rationally when overcome by a mass of raw emotion might have an inkling of how frustrated a baby can feel. Emotions can run away with us, leaving thought processes behind. The resultant chaos may feel so disconcerting that we dissociate.

However, in infancy we have little option. Until greater consciousness develops along with verbal expression, our immature psyche cannot handle and make links with the highly charged sensations our primal energies produce. We are totally dependent on another to nurture and temper them into an organised form. Emotions have yet to interweave with thoughts to form the repertoire of feelings which subsequently underpin every moment of our lives.

∗

The way we are treated as an infant will determine whether we can feel safe in the wider world, particularly in times of great need. It influences all future relationships and is the bedrock for long-term psychic health. The central qualities in this earliest developmental process are acceptance and trust. If found to be wanting, the feelings of insecurity and of low esteem in which the self is held remain, however well defended against, into adulthood.

Taking on the guardianship of a soul when so pliable in infancy is the greatest human privilege. Where a primary carer fails to provide sufficient mirroring and containing, the effect of this early psychic trauma is called the *primal wound* - also known as the *narcissistic wound* as true knowledge and love of self are inhibited.

The desperation a child feels for self affirmation is akin to that when playing 'pass the parcel', once a stalwart at children's birthday parties. This game engenders so much anticipation, hope and frustration and for some, it ends in tears when they are left with just the wrapping. The fate of the narcissistically wounded is similarly sealed for they rarely manage to win their true birth present.

An infant does not come empty into the world. Bountiful gifts to share all round are there for the making and taking, if his carer is sufficiently present to help unpack them. A baby's infectious exuberance may similarly open up his mother's world and awaken her own playful inner child. He is unconsciously as generous as he is demanding. He is naturally uninhibited so will spontaneously express his full gamut of emotions and drives, given half a chance. Ideally, life for him will seem an exciting adventure.

An infant's inner experience at any particular moment becomes for him his total environment which extends endlessly in time. If he feels warm and well fed, then life is blissful. If he is cold and hungry or in pain, all is bad and dangerous and will for ever be so.

These all encompassing absolutes are similar to those experienced when assailed by psychosis. The basic tasks of a child and a psychotic person are similar. Ideally, each needs to come to believe in the healthy reality that life both nourishes and withdraws, creates and destroys, yet renews. Both need to learn to integrate ambivalent forces and find that, rather than their life-force and world be extinguished, they expand.

To help a baby in this work, he needs a consistent mother figure to humanise his instinctual drives and archetypal forces. Acting as a *unifying centre* for his human and divine potential self, she forms a bridging and mediating channel between what is conscious, and what might come into form out of the personal and transpersonal unconscious.

The baby gradually *introjects* this organising principle, in the same way as he learns to fantasise the breast or bottle as a symbol of sustenance and containment. He absorbs his primary carer as a *self/constant object*. Feeling firmly attached, the growing child then more easily tolerates any momentary withdrawal of affection as he can return to a secure base within. In this case, the youngster is well prepared for the next developmental stage towards individuation.

* * *

Section B Self individuation or a self full of shame and fear

We start with the 'both-and' principle in attachment and separation. For a developing baby there are many challenges to be won or lost, and so our study advances to when, at eighteen months or thereabouts, he is impelled to experience and exert his expanding effectiveness.

The time is ripe to start the bumpy stage when toddler challenges parent with such outbursts as, 'No!', 'Me, me, me!' and, eventually, 'Why?' If the child is respected as an intrinsic soul rather than a thing of the parent's own making, such remonstrations will be recognised for what they are - a healthy demonstration of a human's essential need for autonomy. The youngster will not stay in the shadow of his parent.

Of course, even the most emotionally mature parents might not like the way in which he tries to assert himself. But it stands to reason that parents whose sense of selfhood is secure will more easily appreciate and accept their progeny's bid for power. He will be loved despite his recalcitrance.

All parties involved will find this stage of development confusing and trying. (If this is too distant a memory for you, a toddler having a 'strop' in a supermarket might stir old emotions.) This attempt at separating is full of anxiety since a child has to test whether his parents are strong enough and loving enough to bear his fierce hatred and anger as well as his essential need to love and be loved. It is a tough period but of great significance as to whether he is to be autonomous and learn the art of two-way, reasonable communication and compromise.

If successful, this vital experiment will relieve the child of his fear that he could destroy his parents and their love for him. He finds that both they can survive and so can he. He can reconcile confrontation and comfort. The youngster sees in another how both true will and love can coexist and that relationship prevails even when there is a need to exercise individuality. He feels entitled to be, and to live truly. Most of this child will be in the light of his being.

*

Alternatively, there is the 'either-or' principle in attachment and separation. What might happen is that any demanding drive from the developing child is seen as evidence of him having a willful nature; one to be squashed. Whether overtly chastised or ignored for demonstrating signs of self determination, the child's inherent power becomes overlaid with the emotions invoked each time his attempt at self emergence is knocked back. It is a no win situation. The child comes to believe that if he challenges his parents' authority, either they will not survive this raw power or their love for him will not survive, therefore it is unsafe to separate from them. It is either him or them.

In my childhood, any attempt at asserting myself initiated a response from my parents which conveyed the message, 'Who do you think you are!' This message was not a philosophical or rhetorical question, far from it. Rather it was delivered as a shaming and pejorative lashing. Naturally this phrase has become what my *superego* has used to undermine, almost destroy, my entitlement to be my self.

This old message found new ways of creeping inside my head during my run-in with psychosis. For instance, the water pipes at home, in their murmurings, would scold me. Even the moon and stars I called on would hastily retreat behind the clouds to whisper disapprovingly about me and my fate. But, in between psychotic spells, my punitive superego was more succinct and direct in telling me that these aberrations proved just how abnormal and despicable I was. Such crazy behaviour was disgraceful. Surely, I had sunk to the low-life I was made to feel in childhood and was just getting what I deserved.

The superego is an internalised psychic constellation which embraces many authoritative figures. It determines how we feel about ourselves and how we expect other people to see and respond to us. If it majors in the role of judge or critic, whose task is to sublimate our urge for autonomy of self using fear and shame, it will keep rubbing salt into our primal wound.

For me, dealing with this critical, persistent and silencing voice inside my head is an ongoing task, particularly as I write about it. However, having found the '*autistic* inner child' who was once locked behind the door to my unconscious, I believe in what she has to offer. I know that out of the dark horrors of psychosis can come enlightening feelings and thoughts.

Now, I can retranslate the denigrating and mocking monologue of 'Who do you think you are!', into an interested inquiry as to who might I think I am. A more reasonable and empathic dialogue is developing between this inner persecutory authority and my emerging truth. So I am finding deep within me that there is a self I value, one who is entitled to take a place in the world and have a voice.

*

Where there is self awareness, there can be shame of that self. While fear is the most powerful and primitive element in living creatures, shame is soul destroying. It strikes at the core of our existence and can anesthetise memory of our inborn connection to source, both spiritual and personal.

In early infancy, when there is little consciousness of self, our sensory antennae are hypersensitive and we are particularly open to the subliminal world. Within the common boundary of a primary relationship, conscious and unconscious emotions and thoughts are easily transferred. We identify with mother and thereby the base of our superego is formed.

There is no time that we are more susceptible to introjecting shaming messages than when we are very young. As well as verbal, facial and body language, at a more latent energetic level we will sense if our nursing mother is ashamed of her flowing breast; or whether our fierce need to satiate hunger elicits in her the same fear we might feel of devouring or being devoured. Each of us may feel full of shame and fear, so empty and starved of real love.

Certain methods of toilet training are loaded with telltale signs of how, by inducing shame, we are disciplined to perform and feel in life. Such associations to our natural physical functions, including sexual, often manifest in self hatred, disgust or self loathing. While loathing suggests that there is attacking rage, disgust indicates extreme repulsion, a moving away from what we and others are composed of and are. Two-way contamination is an issue in psychosis also, when there is confusion between the elemental forces outside and those inside, and what is harmful and what is creative.

When little, if it seems unsafe to offload our troublesome emotions, we come to believe that what we feel must be dangerous. Thus primal energy remains largely unintegrated, unrefined and unresolved and becomes the origin of physical, psychological and behavioural problems. What needs to be amalgamated into the intrinsic self keeps fermenting. Indeed, when shame and fear continually stalk us, we may be inhibited to the extent that our inner substance does, eventually, mushroom into madness.

*

Shame and fear stand in the light of being the unique human soul we are and therefore may shade how we respond to what is written here. This is because all emotion arising out of transgressions against us in our formative years will be laden with shame and fear. They radically reduce our power to influence the world so we can become impotent victims and correspondingly might retaliate violently.

Shame and fear are not tools which create a law abiding society. They are central weapons in the cause and effect of civil disobedience and mental disorder. They arrest the natural development of our core essence and a framework to balance emotions. Then, if an inner conflict increases above a certain intensity or our outer world is too challenging, we will easily fragment back to the bundle of primal energy we were in early infancy. The destructive superego and its allies, shame and fear, can be seen to have done their worst.

Hallucinations, delusions and violent attacks on others are often reconstituted replays of the original obstruction to the birth of our core self. All normal avenues of connection and expression, once more, seem cut off to us. Murderous rage, along with the agony of shame and terror of having been thrown out of the heavenly bliss of *symbiotic* union with archetypal mother, rampages around and within us.

Unlike anger, which is provoked by something evident and so has an object of direction, rage stems from the stimulation of emotional memories originating from the abnegation of self. It can blast through when we feel humiliated and are desperate to establish some sort of contact with another. There again, rage can be overriden by fear of further shame and thus is apparent only in the way we crush our precious self. Rage is diffused and 'confused' with the deepest and fiercest of far-reaching energies. All these emotions can lie seething in the turmoil of our unconscious and produce mental instability.

Some of us act out this emotional *splitting* off of what was deemed not good, right or important, by seeking retribution for our own painful downfall. Many remain dissociated. Others return to this unintegrated material, by going mad. Whatever way, just as our essential self was rejected, branded bad by hot searing shame, so we become down and outcast from society once again.

Much of what society considers to be bad, even evil behaviour in the world, stems from how individuals were made to feel unacceptable, perhaps wicked, in childhood through their carer using shaming and frightening methods of repression. Rather than leave themselves open to more abuse, they hide their vulnerability and neediness with rage, sometimes with violence. For example, a child who is hit by his carer, when he steps out of line, may be more inclined to go on to commit grievous bodily harm. This observation is not to justify criminal behaviour but to highlight the need for carers to gain emotional maturity.

There is an underlying fear of the primal forces and thus of children becoming little 'savages' if unrestrained. The psychopath or *sociopath* can function without any self awareness. He experiences, therefore, no guilt or shame and neither sees the effect of, nor takes responsibility for, his lack of discipline and antisocial behaviour.

On the other hand, a child in his egocentricity often feels responsible for everybody's welfare and believes that he alone is the cause of all positive and negative experiences in his environment. The child's grandiose sense of being, both supremely powerful and extremely powerless, needs clear and careful handling. The same goes for the person experiencing these absolutes in psychosis. This difficult task will be further addressed.

*

A child needs to test his strength of form and to feel some clear defining edges. But often, he dare not express his narcissistic rage at an assault on his being. Anyway, he cannot afford to feel that his primary carer is negligent and bad. Better for him to carry the blame and shame, to believe that he is the one who is deficient.

In idealising his carer, however, he devalues himself and forms an enduring split which is the basis of madness. Unable to freely respond, his real self becomes increasingly worthless.

You might know a youngster who is withdrawn or too good to be true so that the 'tiny tot tantrum time' passes unnoticed. His will to experiment, make mistakes and develop in his own way has been subdued and he remains anxiously attached. He is merely a caste of what his carers want him to be. For him, love is synonymous with obedience.

Another reaction to a shaming, suffocating, disinterested or dictatorial parent is for a child to come to believe that the only way to survive is to fight. A child will use any means to be noticed. At least his anger has an effect on people which wards off feelings of helplessness and non existence. Society is bound to pay attention to a rebellious youngster who behaves as if the world is against him. For him, power is synonymous with aggression.

While anger can be useful for pushing people away and thereby clearing space for the true self to develop, without the support of real love, only a sense of inner emptiness will be growing in that fought for space. When there is nowhere to consciously channel both love and will, a child surrenders true aliveness for a survival state.

An oppressive regime, or indeed an unholding environment, is not conducive to transforming a child's drives and emotions into feelings which he can articulate and demonstrate appropriately. Dialogue with dynamically opposing emotions, external and internal, will not be promoted. Without an empathic bond with his core being, a child will not feel the joy, sadness and many emotional strands which make up the fabric of life. He is simply not 'all there'. There is little loving relationship between his primary carer and what is real in him.

An infant might not be able to activate ideal parental care for his essential self, but he can certainly prod his carers' primal wounds. Then, two-way communication will be fraught with feelings of helplessness and neediness. A phenomenal amount of energy exists between child and carer for every aspect - physical, emotional, mental and spiritual - joins in the battle for life in this vital relationship.

A youngster's primitive thrust for self expression demands satisfaction and this can bring a resurgence of his carers' unassimilated and therefore unevolved, primal forces. Some parents have no frame of reference to draw on. The repressed emotions from their past are attributed to the present. Their offspring, therefore, is seen as the instigator of their discomfort, the challenger of their fragile sense of capability and the bearer of elements which must be annihilated. The carers cannot stand the internal pressure, so take it out on the child. Thus the history of abuse gets handed down.

At last the parents have a sense of power over the weak and helpless child out there, rather than with their own neglected being, within. They cannot help themselves. Pay back time. Obviously such retribution is often unwittingly carried out as, without access to their own original pain, they are unaware that they are hurting their young. For some parents, no memory of receiving loving care and security when they needed consoling comes to their rescue. They remain dissociated.

When a carer masks his feelings of inadequacy, which have been sparked by his child's total dependency, with angry and shaming retaliation, then fear, rejection and shame can become inextricably bound up with the need for affection. In this type of attachment, it is not love which binds. The core of the narcissistic wound remains trapped by neediness because many adults feel too ashamed and fearful of admitting, and even more of exhibiting, any vulnerability. Their superego derides them for not having grown up and of being inherently weak.

Parents are so used to riding roughshod over their own fearful and shameful part, having themselves been humiliated in this way, they can dish out the same almost as if it is expedient and their right to inflict what they received. It often brings a sadistic satisfaction to those who have been similarly mistreated. Using degrading and frightening tactics to 'knock a child into shape' is misguided. But such punitive authority can be defensively rationalised as being essential learning. 'It didn't do me any harm', is a favourite retort. By trivializing their child's emotions and demeaning him, they feel better about themselves.

※

As a child, so often we take responsibility for a symptom of our family disorder. Along with our primary carer's coaching, the role any siblings play can also determine what part we are apportioned in the family system, whether as carer, scapegoat, rebel, high achiever or an amalgam of many. We develop an adapted self in order to safeguard some equilibrium in both our internal and external milieu. What is more extraordinary is that even a problem which originates in a previous generation, about which nobody seems to know, may get picked up by us and we try to resolve it. (see www.movingconstellations.com)

This was true for a young City financier who came to me weighed down with excess baggage, the texture of which seemed to arise from a deep sadness in the family which nobody owned. My client's mother needed him to make her happy. Apparently, his father could not bear any sign of suffering or vulnerability and therefore overcompensated with a strict, driving work ethic and also set up huge sibling rivalry in his children's many sporting pursuits. The father's grandeur was reflected in their shining trophies.

My client was sensitive to and affected by the family's inadmissible feelings, but he kept smiling. His way of bonding with his family would be curtailed if he was successful in his own right. Here was a man who took the hard road to prove how strong he was, trying to please all and sundry so that he might receive accolades for his caring ways and business accomplishments - until the dam burst and he began to grieve for his own lost inner child. He dropped out of the 'rat race' and in time, found his true orientation and vocation.

Siblings are treated differently often according to gender. It is not unusual for a son to be encouraged by a parent to fight, to 'be a man' and not show any tenderness. The worst possible sin is to be a 'wimp'. The same parent might chastise a daughter for being a tomboy and for displaying any aggressive traits. Being a 'doormat' exemplifies the ideal female and standing up for her self is inherently bad.

What is considered to be bad by one parent, however, might be perceived very differently by the other, which is very muddling for the child who is trying to accommodate both. But when the same parent gives conflicting messages, it is more than confusing, it is enough to make a child feel crazy.

※

'To be or not to be, that is the question?' - or, is it a question of grandiosity versus shame. At this juncture it must be said that a toddler's burgeoning egotism may well need moderating, since too much is conducive to madness as is too little.

While an illusion of narcissistic splendour is vital to start with, this second developmental stage requires that a mother reduces her total commitment to her child. The irony is that if by some miracle a mother knew exactly what her youngster was feeling and accurately responded to his every need, why would he bother to individuate? She needs to empathically 'fail' occasionally and be just '*good enough*'. Having felt supremely omnipotent through the attachment to this powerful other, the undifferentiated child can but contract into a smaller self. But he needs to be gently led to the painful truth that mother is neither infallible nor just part of himself.

For a youngster, forming a boundary which delineates identity is essential, if he is to make his true way in life. In his struggle for independence, he has to meet another's limits, and his own. While a child needs to find the difference between his fantastical self and other, can this be achieved without his natural creativity becoming saddled and reigned in by shame?

Rather than a youngster's grandiosity be stamped on, it may be channelled into a grand sense of aliveness and potential fulfillment of self. Surely it is better for a child to be flushing and filling with pride than blushing and cringing with shame. Self consciousness expands joyfully when praised and painfully when shamed.

Being proud of who he is, a child more easily accommodates the fact that he needs other people to flourish around him also. He will see his particular portion in the overall order of things. From here, he can progress ... until, next stop, he is the stroppy teenager. Out of a robust emotional world, he becomes his own person and takes his rightful place in life without his primary carer.

As children, we need to learn to resolve the conflict

between our assertive self and our authoritative carer, through the cycles of rupture and repair. Thereby we prevent internal contradictory emotions becoming split off within ourselves and a negative-positive sense of self and other. The way we deal with ambivalent feelings in our family becomes the working model of how as adults we relate to our self and to humanity in general.

When we can cope with both loving and hating someone, without feeling shame or fear, we are on the road to emotional maturity. Sadly the 'both-and' principle is still a challenge to many of us adults. This difficult and ongoing task is pivotal in our psychological welfare.

*

It might be helpful to extrapolate the two strands of shame, and to separate shame from the feelings of guilt.

Guilt is about an action we have committed, for which we can be punished, forgiven, even exonerated. It can make us feel contrite for what we have done or said. Whereas a 'guilt trip' is self defeating and indulgent if prolonged, the prick of conscience is an instrument for change, for learning from our mistakes and making amends.

Shame, however, is about who we are. If caught by the barbed hook of shame implanted by our primary carers, it is a toxic shame as it is contaminated by their conscious and unconscious material. But in taking the lid off this dysfunctional shame, we may reach another sort of shame. Only when we are untrue to our intrinsic self, when we let our self really down - the ultimate betrayal - might we feel true and healthy shame. Even then, our self worth is not abnegated.

However, our primary carer is responsible for introducing us to a sense of guilt for conduct which might harm us and/or others. The occasional reprimand or punishment for obnoxious behaviour coupled with care and an explanation are the maxims of 'tough love'.

As a child, we need to learn that we will not always get our way if we cry, shout, demand, grab, lash out and generally run amok. Yet, acting out in this way is a symptom of our basic lust for life and chastising us for having this impulse degrades what is inherent in us. Eliciting shame for the emotional self is not a good recipe for exercising self mastery over our emotions and conduct. Shame castrates and strips us of confidence. Guilt, on the other hand, encourages us to check our primitive impulses, but not ignore them, so that we realise our true nature and take responsibility for our actions.

If chided for our emotions, we feel dismissed. Either we will withdraw and close down or try and demonstrate our unhappiness by upsetting another. Both reactions only further alienate us from people, whereas respectful honesty can liberate and produce peace in our self and the environment.

A message which invokes guilt for what we do, rather than shame for who we are, might sound something like this - 'I love you, so rather than shout and hurt your baby sister, please tell me what you really feel upset about, then we might sort it out'. Although admonished for demonstrating our raw feelings inappropriately, we are assured that, as a person, we are still acceptable.

✻

When encouraged to explore with another our dependency needs and primitive drives, we realise that our emotions can be tolerated and managed. By assimilating and refining these early in life, our intrinsic qualities can be used expediently and we will similarly honour the sacredness in other human beings. Instead of being hidebound by shame and fear, we will exercise self discipline and with it, mental balance.

Correspondingly, when our primary carer models a way of expressing emotions appropriately, we will naturally internalise a balanced code of conduct. Of course, as we develop into an autonomous being, we will formulate our particular view on life and can dismantle or build on this early foundation. Then a feeling of true shame, not instilled by another, will be induced when we fail to keep integrity with our core values. Thereby we forge a healthy conscience and inhibit destructive behaviour which makes for a truly humane society.

These platitudes sound so very righteous. Taking the high and moral ground is so easy when talking about shame yet, heaven forbid that I might be delivering words of condemnation, as if from a pulpit, for not being able to achieve such perfection. It is not my intention to engender shame in anyone, as it stifles the ability to remain open to what is positive here. If you come from a shame-based, primary family system and in reading this appraisal you are filling up with shame or using angry denial to protect yourself from it, let me temper this. Have no doubt, these ideas come from not only my studies, discussions, observations and professional experience, but also from my memories of how I fell short in mothering my two children. If only I knew then what I know now. As it was, my mother and father were crippled by shame so I took on this mantle and passed it on to my children.

Maybe a pause is in order here, while you consider your own familial set up. What particular aspects hit home, so far? Of course, it takes more than a few minutes to extricate our self from the mass of early material we have absorbed - as our whole way of thinking, feeling and acting has been designed by it - but it would be useful to give it a go.

* * *

Section C Seeking clarity

Keeping up appearances was my family's fundamental creed. Ours was a 'nice' family. But however hard I tried to disguise my shameful faults, I never felt good enough. This discoloured everything I did and was.

Having to cover up our truth means that there is no congruence between our words and feelings. Our internal dialogue, often still encoded in our body, has no bearing on what actually comes out of our mouths. When little, we are particularly susceptible to picking up such discrepancies in our carers. It is a lasting gift when carers are honest with their feelings and likewise value and encourage their child's different feelings to develop and be expressed.

On the contrary, I was told how I was feeling. 'This feels good and makes you happy', seemed to tag all that came my way which was bewildering as, deep inside, it did not feel good.

So I clung onto some sanity by believing it must be me who was wrong and bad. I took the situation for granted as I knew no other.

While just a withering look of displeasure or brief withdrawal of attention from a carer can train a child into submission, extreme and extended shaming methods of control can cancel out all consciousness, which is the mechanism of repression and a format for mental illness. This is why, ultimately, essential facets of our self may be discovered in our psychoses.

Shame is a two-edged sword as it separates us from our self and carves us up into pieces, thereby stoking mental derangement. It is an ideal instrument of administering pain as, unlike a physical blow, its source is not easily discernible, neither does it leave a visible scar. Shame cuts the deepest of hidden wounds - it twists and turns into the very heart of our being. Many remain in fear of recollecting the agony of such penetrating shame.

If there is no one to turn to who registers our true existence, trauma can open wide our inner caretaking structure. In Lewis Carroll's classic, Alice tried to make sense out of Wonderland but found herself asking, *'Who in the world am I then?'* When we cannot see the logic in what is happening around us, it will be like trying to work out a jigsaw puzzle when blindfold. Where do we begin?

Even if someone comes into our life who does hear what we truly feel and treats us as an individual, whether in childhood or adulthood, what often happens is that such reliability disorientates us still further. Having endeavoured to create some sense of order out of disorder, we still see our new surroundings through our old crazed lens because we need to preserve a constancy of self experience.

Therefore we disprove what might well be a good and wholesome experience by spoiling it. However tortuous our crazy internalised realm might be, it is central to understanding our self. Breaking the code and facing a new reality feels even more threatening. The charm of dependency protects us from the horror of reality.

A dysfunctional family system can look ostensibly close and caring. Its appearance is deceptive yet often sustained, as no one wants to confront the unwholesome truth. In such a milieu, a child is emotionally affected whether the abuse is directed at him, his siblings or a caregiver. Indeed, the more indirect the insult, the more difficult it is to confront and realise its effect. The obscure is harder to symbolise and verbalise and thereby to manifest an aspect in response. The child has little hope of standing back and making sense of the system he is caught in. Accessing the memory and effecting change in adulthood will be similarly difficult.

The primal wound exemplifies the covert nature of emotional abuse. A primary carer's narcissistic needs are often too abhorrent to be conscious and the attempt to satisfy them through amenable family members is interpreted as love - but it is a hollow token. While staying in a *co-dependent* setup seems to be in everyone's best interest, the child is not rightly served and remains confused and unsatisfied. In such a honey trap, love can be laced with severely damaging elements which the carer cannot abide in him/herself.

For the child, it is like taking his fill from a golden chalice full of poisoned nectar. After drinking this brew, it takes a while before the effect kicks in. Sometimes he never fathoms out how he came to feel so bad. He has no excuse to feel anything other than gratitude.

In the early years, we have no firm basis for our reality if our carers' messages and rewards for pleasing them are polluted, contradictory and unpredictable. Without a certain degree of constancy and congruence, we cannot trust what we think and feel, neither can we resolve what is denied so that conflicting aspects come into any rapprochement. There is a massive gulf between what seems to be and what actually is.

*

If both our parents are insufficient, it is easier to split them into one who is 'good' and see the other as 'bad'. The most common solution is for the man to be viewed as bad. A male's power is generally more overt than a female's. We were born of a woman and more often are fed by one. Our survival depends on her so we have to trust her, even to the detriment of self.

We tuck our frustrating, angry or absent mother figure into the shadow so that we can make out that we are safe. It is easy to pretend all's well if primed to ignore our own pain, when we have abandoned our authentic emotional self. Mum's the word.

We like to hold onto an idealised picture of the archetypal mother and infant, that once upon a time, we felt the blissful state of being loved unconditionally and joyously held in safety. Such a fantasy compensates for, and masks, the feelings of fear, shame, rage and pain if our true being was neglected.

Reports of child abuse are shocking enough. But if it is a woman who has beaten, or has sexually or emotionally violated, a child, then this headline-grabbing news is greeted with horror and disbelief. It is too awful to think that a female is capable of carrying out such deeds. This ultimate taboo challenges our picture of who we ourselves were part of and our much needed perception of a mother's gentle and loving nature - the female gives not takes life.

My mother's pain was all too tangible to me. But acknowledging what was negative in my mother, upon whose image I was dependent and who depended on my allegiance, would shatter my illusion of security. For me to have a continuing sense of existence, I had to keep my internal myth alive. Surely mother was adorable.

It took many years and much soul searching, before I realised that I had been kidding myself my entire life, ever since I was too small and innocent to know any better. Coming to accept her shortcomings has been hard.

On the other hand, my father's hatred and anger towards me was more direct and obvious, and so less easily denied by me. When my father was 80 years old, he told my mother that, because I had shunned him on his return from the war, he felt quite entitled to reject me thereafter. I was only eighteen months old at the time. Naturally, I had felt threatened by this strange intruder and, in witnessing me clinging to my mother, he would have been reminded of his unmet primal needs. Try as I may, forever after, I could never heal the rift which came from this moment when my father felt rejected by me. It is sad we shared such depths of pain but could never speak of it openly.

My father was more involved in my sister's development. Initially he created a protective boundary around his wife and child. Then, as my sister grew older, he acted as a wedge between what was a potentially suffocating mother-child dyad. She also had more flesh on her as protective cladding and erected a wall of anger to ward off my mother's attempt to possess her.

Unlike my sister, I never developed such insulation. Looking back on my childhood now, it is easy to see how I failed to draw an essential boundary between my mother and myself. It was an emotional quagmire. But for a long time in therapy I was not able to grasp the substance of my relationship with her. It slipped silkily, slimily through my hands.

But just as psychosis was taking hold, our unhealthy enmeshment became more evident. In what felt like a waking dream, I saw myself surrounded by *primordial* reptiles. One was snapping at my heels – surely my father – but another seemed more deadly as it was exuding green slime which was insidiously covering and entering my body. Subsequently, whenever emotions associated with my mother came up, it felt as if this substance was enfolding me. The more I fought to disentangle myself, the more tightly it clung on.

When young I found that slipping into this seemingly sweet jelly was safer than standing out as a target in the open or being ignored by my mother. Green jelly to children can look and feel so good. It slides down easily into hungry mouths.

Once I had connected to the after-effects of such ingestion in psychosis, I became increasingly alert to people with deceptively pernicious ways - and they stopped showing up in my life. This is not magic, just the laws of nature. The way that I learnt to survive in childhood had well and truly outlived its usefulness.

I know now that my mother's invasive qualities left an indelible mark on my psyche. But being wrapped up in love, they were difficult to recognise.

*

It is challenging to find out home truths, whether we have idealised or denigrated our caretakers. Like others, bearing in mind my parents' background, they did the best they could by bringing me up in the only way they knew. Yet allegiance does not absolve our primary carers' mistakes, neither does renouncing them rectify or assuage the pain and distress of realising that they were not perfect. Digging up the dirt of the past and casting it at others is no long term solution to healing a blighted life. However, facing up to who we and others really are, can ultimately allow genuine relationships to develop, even with parents who fell short in their job of nurturing us.

Some never take a second glance at their early psychic development; they are careless of their self unfoldment. Well meaning people say, 'Don't look back, look forward' and that we should 'Put the past behind us where it belongs'. Ultimately this is so. But by looking at our shadow, we can find what is behind most of our current problems.

For some of us, all the old messages founded on 'should', 'don't you dare', 'not good enough', have resulted in our feeling that something is missing in our life. Finding the root cause of our *psychopathology*, which literally means 'understanding the suffering of soul', can ease the shame, fear and hate of our core self which we have taken on board.

By looking at, rather than through, the lenses prescribed in childhood, we might see how distorted our outlook and responses have been. By examining what stifled my original perceptions, I began to unclog my visual pathways of 'green slime' and I glimpsed a new angle on many things which had been so skewed in my life. As old images became more transparent, I could more readily distinguish between outdated perceptions and present reality. It was like stepping into a different world.

As children, we did not have all the facts with which to make a considered choice. We were dependent on our parents for our emotional and physical sustenance and also for confirming our perceptions. As adults, our perspective on life is still restricted by these introjects. To come into alignment with our true self, we have to reconcile these adopted ways of seeing with our own way of being. At the time of our wounding, we made a packaged deal with life. Now we have the chance to undo it and reconfigure our outlook.

But it takes more than a shift in perspective in order for long-term healing to take place. As well as becoming mindful as to the naked facts of how our truth was first disavowed, we also need to awaken our frozen core.

We can remain anaesthetised to the pain from our primal wound, therefore real pleasure, for the rest of our life. How sad that would be. Or, we may go back, beyond any depression or anger, into the darkest well of sadness. By mourning for what was missing in our past, which we can never have, we might make room for our future. Either we relinquish our yearning for an ideal mother figure or we will be forever seeking another to fulfill our unmet needs - and how many of us can honestly say we have never hoped for that.

But it is no good wringing our hands and brooding over what life has dealt us. This is not what self analysis is all about. We cannot change what happened to us when we were little. But we may stir compassion for what in us was thwarted and hurt and thereby reclaim our full feeling self who was denied.

Only by rekindling our still powerful, unevolved sensations and emotions, which have endured in the darkest chamber of our unconscious and on which all current 'issues' are based, will we feel truly comfortable in our skin. This takes a brave heart but in this very painful but essential process, we start to re-parent our self.

*

In my case, my early environment was so unclear that I could only untangle my self by regressing to this time in later years and by integrating the madness that such ambiguity had left in its shadowy wake.

I tried to live up to the expectations of my parents whose overriding criteria for life was to be presentable. Image was all. My defensive mechanism to ward off showing and fully feeling my needy self included a grandiose perfectionism while the delicate, fallible self was trodden down in contempt.

But when in late adulthood I came to realise, more fully, the real emotional interplay going on behind the scenes, this 'superior' persona crumbled and I disappeared into the psychotic chaos of my once split off, disorganised and unprocessed material. It was horrendous existing alone in this dimension. But I had to cut off from outer reality, I now realise, as the possibility of re-experiencing the full impact of the searing shame and pain of my original separation from self was too awful.

In a manner of speaking, I had taken off my emotional underwear. The garment of decency which covered my naked self was in rags. I felt stripped to the bone. Such was my fear of ridicule and rejection, the shame of contempt, that when eventually I did dare expose my natural impulses towards my therapist, laced with fury and distress, I cringed. I expected him to be furious and repelled by what was, essentially, my neediness.

My adapted self had given way to these once inadmissible, mortifying but real feelings, yet rather than reinforce this psychic split, he encouraged them to stay active. Thus, having survived the onslaught of the very worst in myself, the energy which I had replicated into entities did not retreat into the shadows from whence it came. Instead, gradually, I built up a tolerance of these natural forces. The psychic door to my hitherto primitive unconscious was kept open, although many years passed before I could let any of my therapist's empathic response filter through.

There is a huge need for recognition and love in all those who hide a deep primal wound, which is fiercely felt when this is open and bleeding. It is the finest blessing when we can acknowledge our neediness to someone and come to realise that they are not out to shame us, then compassion and care for our wounded self grows within us. It takes just one person.

This communion is so extreme that I can only liken it to being a convict on Death Row and knowing that someone, outside the prison walls, is aware of our existence. Liberation is possible when we realise that loving acceptance awaits us; that in our raw rage and blind terrorised state we can be met with enough respectful warmth and light. For it is for our long lost self to find its own way out. Having been incarcerated years ago, we can but wait patiently for what is unknown within to come without, into the unknown.

The source of madness is an absence of a strong centre

(which we will talk about more in Chapter 6), and shame is the prison warder which keeps the true self bound. If our primary carer judged our real self unfit for social inclusion, our exacting superego will continue to enforce this life sentence. It will keep us locked into negative belief systems by applying the chief antagonist to freely becoming who we truly are - namely shame. Of course, our superego was learning the tricks of the trade when we were very young, so it knows just where our weakest points are. It can cut us down to size and when we are at our most vulnerable, it goes in for the kill.

Over time, it is enough to drive us crazy. For example, lack of friends or a job might bring impoverishment and sadness. However, if tied up with shame, we feel we are not important, wanted or good enough, often all three and more besides, so we might slip into severe depression or another mental disorder.

✱

While we can stay paralysed in fear, fight or fly in the face of fear, however hard we try to hide our face in shame, shame gnaws at our heart causing the deepest of primal wounds. Shame continually eats away at our insides, like corrosive acid, until there is little left of us. It can eliminate all sense of who we truly are. Then however 'good' we appear to be to our primary carers and later in life to the rest of the world, we know that, at a deep level inside, there are emotions and thoughts which our punitive superego considers bad – we are our own worst enemy.

Where there is shame, there is always a 'should' lurking around somewhere - we should be different. We might catch our superego out and reframe 'should' into 'could', which gives us choice. But the self-lacerating superego can cut us to ribbons by trumping this with a real double whammy and make us feel ashamed of feeling ashamed.

We just cannot win. Having a critical superego will mean that we compare ourselves unfavourably with others and try and adapt our self accordingly. Then how we present ourselves to those we want approval and love from, is not the real us. Although some people might be canny enough to see behind our persona and still care for us, we may not feel this. Our experience is that who we truly are is not recognised and loved at all.

Such is the power of shame, it can contaminate and cover the totality of our vital essence. At an elemental level we feel that we are to be despised. If we were born the 'wrong' gender, shape or colour, were conceived 'by mistake' and unwanted, then we feel damned from the start. Shame is a curse. We form a survivor personality principally to cover our shame of who we are.

Starting with the original sin of Adam and Eve, some religions construe that we are a shameful manifestation of this act. Whatever the joy and pride in which we may be conceived and born, even if we rationally disagree with such doctrines, often we remain steeped in these edicts.

*

Do we have the will to free our self from the tyranny of existential shame which is cultivated in many of us?

Will, in its pure, loving and powerful form, is fed by soul. But will can be forceful and self defeating in a superego's hands. It seems that only strict discipline or rage is a match for a punitive superego - but this is not so.

A friend, dear to my heart, is so sensitive to any hint of a 'should' that the mildest suggestion from another will bring down the iron shutters and he does the very opposite. It might seem that we can counteract a controlling superego by banishing it to the shadows - but this is not possible.

Sometimes our superego has been reinforced by an imposing and punishing god. Extreme suffering might be seen as a blessed sign as to our worthiness for divine salvation, which perpetuates the wretched masochist. Such an all encompassing superego can make us feel so small that we inflate ourselves, not with anger, but with purity or mystical qualities. Denial of baser elements can mean that we become over self righteous. False pride is the other side of false shame and they meet each other at the critical point of the superego. It feels as if the superego which demands perfection can only be faced by a magnificent superhuman being - but this is not the solution.

I have tried all these angles. But what brought me the vibrant strength and clarity to match, sometimes outflank and disarm, my commanding superego, was owning up to what was buried inside me. What had kept my adapted self in line for years, only had a hold on me while I was afraid and ashamed of my inherent nature. Thus my superego came to form a coalition with my, once thwarted, life-giving energy. Now it is gently transforming into a companionable, sustaining and quiet inner authority which no longer needs to follow, or negate, my parents' codes.

Without the fear of shameful exposure, the fuller and surer we will feel. We can assert our will without aggrandising our self with hostility or perfectionism. The more we embrace the reality of our self and are honest with others, the less anxiety we will have about being 'found out'. What a load off our minds!

At the depths of my being, in the mass of psychotic material, lay a soul agent for truth which was ultimately life enhancing; an inner knowing, a guiding voice coming from my real heart's desire and wisdom. Now I can but follow my deepest calling, my reason for being born. Of course, such a commitment still arouses some fear and shame of failure and rejection. But being released from an overly restrictive superego, most of the time, I feel I am 'enough' which, in turn, enables me to naturally unfold and develop my potential.

Here you might wish to draw breath, ponder on the foregoing ideas presented and consider which do and which do not resonate with you. With these in mind, in the next chapter we can address how we repeat the patterns laid down in childhood and how we might change this early conditioning.

*

Chapter 5

A Formation of Repeating Patterns

Section A Reproducing our primary relationships and environment

Generally, patterns of behaviour and ways of relating to others, set up in the first few years of life, remain with us into adulthood. We know the codes by heart and it is in the affairs of the heart that this early imprinting may be most apparent. Therefore we begin this chapter by focusing on how our primary and adult relationships often follow suit.

If we are a woman and our father was physically and emotionally unavailable, chances are we will fall for every guy who is distant, is married and/or is a misogynist. If we are a man, we may seek the company of males who are as cold as our father. Whatever our gender, if our mother expected us to fulfill her narcissistic needs, we will probably attract female friends and partners who are oblivious to our needs. It is not that we make a conscious choice to repeat what is familiar, but those who really love us just do not appeal.

How can we account for this? The fundamental problem is that because we still yearn to fulfill our unmet primal needs, we are often drawn to people who present the same challenge of relationship which we faced in early childhood. Nevertheless, we tell ourselves that this time we might just get it right and so win what we missed out on the first time around. The pull is irresistible.

We wish to be loved for who we genuinely are, yet if

we have no emotional access to our authentic self, we cannot let such loving attention come close. Neither is it possible to love another from this true place. Repeatedly we recreate situations wherein our lack of self love is mirrored back to us.

Unconsciously we re-stage the circumstances of our early wounding which evoke our unresolved emotions and *complexes*. In this way, we keep picking at our primal wound to achieve the neurotic feelings that we have become attached to. We can but keep to our well rehearsed life script. With the immutable laws of affinity, we attract people who are inclined to put us in the position that we are used to and so in a perverse way feels comfortable. Compelling entanglements draw on the ropes we learnt to weave as a child.

Being easily seduced by what 'could be', we manage to sustain our idealising dreams if given just a smidgen of affection. Hope springs eternal that a partner may provide what we did not receive when young. But the truth is, nobody can placate this gnawing need in any lasting way. While it can be fun looking for our knight in shining armour or for an adoring angel to rescue us, they can turn out to be, aided and abetted by us, the devil in disguise. An illusional, yet vicious circle, is often created.

What appears to be love can be issues of neediness, fear, sex, power and, conditioning. Either we stay in the world of make-believe, or we master the remote control which pushes our buttons - the emotional pressure points which make us play out our early history - and we wake up to reality.

✷

There again, we might try and buck the system – no way do we want to end up like our parents. We gather around us work mates, friends and lovers who epitomise everything that they were not, or that they disapproved of.

The trouble is, if we keep defying old directives as a *reactive formation* against early authority, we are no more making choices from a free and genuine place than one who persistently conforms. By continuing to operate from the effect of others, we will still find the same dynamics developing which we experienced in our formative years - whether we felt forced into a position of opposition, of stubborn resistance or of compliance.

This 'repetition compulsion' further cements our life script in that things can only be the way we have been led to believe. Yet, while everyone else seems to be running the show, we are the ones who have set up our well known scenarios - even when we think we wish fervently for something else.

It is a ghastly shock to wake up one day and think, 'Now where have I heard that before – that's just what my dad used to say', and, 'Goodness gracious me, I'm in bed with my mum!' The myth of *Oedipus* is continually being played out. The cycles in generations grind on regardless. The endearing comment, 'You are just like your Aunt Maud,' no longer might be heard when taking tea in the drawing room; the beverage, place and name may have changed and our aunt's blue rinse replaced by a shock of red hair, but the game is the same.

Our family members really know how to get to us. Some years ago, I was in Kew Gardens with my son and daughter and was admiring some sculptures. But the two of them were spoiling my enjoyment as they kept metaphorically prodding each other, until eventually, the younger was flattened into a sulk. So familiar was my reaction to their squabbling that I felt cast back in time. I literally had to turn and check that I was not still with my five and three year old children. But no - two thirty-plus adults were walking either side of me.

Infuriatingly, it is not just when we are with our kith and kin that we engage in such interaction. We see our primary family in every Tom, Dick and Harriet and eventually get them to play the different parts out for us so that we can carry on in our own customary role. We dance a *'folie à deux'*, a perfected art-form which mesmerises us, with our partner, family, friends, colleagues, even strangers. This can become such a tightly choreographed performance that we no longer know any alternative steps to take towards another.

Family systems have such a vital hold on us. Even when we are old enough to know better and we think that we have made our own way in the world, we find the same scenarios keep happening all over again. They have in mine. For instance, I was attracted to a college which, in my experience, operated out of a shame-based family system. Most members of this narcissistic organisation hid their lack of true self under a refined mask and apparel.

Anyone not colluding in this cover up would find himself a 'persona non grata'. Few dared see what was paraded before them, and it took me a long while to dissolve such psychic fog so that I formed this view. There was a rule, unspoken of course, of 'I won't tell if you won't'. Maintaining this fantasy was essential to their collective survival. But in this place safety was an illusion. It was veiled in intoxicating love which was as deadly as methane gas. I had to break the spell which bound me.

Disenchantment requires a terrific amount of hard work rather than any magical divining because the stronger the magnetism, and paradoxically the repulsion, the more likely we are to be facing what has been unacknowledged in our self. So while we do not have to remain stuck in a relationship or situation which is not good for us, we can acknowledge such a 'fatal attraction' for the teaching it may bring. Can we bless the re-enactment of our familiar dynamic, re-frame it as an opportunity to re-form our patterning?

*

A driven need for the familiar can get out of hand. Filling up our diary with a chain of events and significant people brings some cohesion, reliability and organisation in our life. But we can become so identified with, and dependent on, external objects that we may turn into a control freak in an effort to hold ourselves and our world together. Even when we moan about the daily grind, having carried our burdensome and now redundant patterns for so long, we cannot let all our hard effort go to waste. Despite such investment causing us to miss out on so much, we live by ingrained laws which stultify our growth but we are reluctant to cast them aside.

What holds us back from forging new pathways are the shackles of our prescribed adaptations, and correspondingly the lack of a secure connection to a genuine feeling self. Without such a centre, we dare not step out of our habitual way of carrying on. Our life revolves around the status quo.

Being rooted in the rut of conditioned responses is like being stuck in the groove of a worn down record, circling round getting nowhere, never reaching the hole in our centre. We cling onto our deeply embedded belief system. But the momentum to keep orbiting around a laid down construction which is not our own means that we never catch up with our true self.

Watching a dog chasing its tail is always amusing. My father chased round in circles, although it was not funny being caught up in this whirl of activity. When he retired to Spain, he was still driven as a slave to a rigid routine. Having attended to his domestic chores in the morning, he would then venture off in his car. At two o'clock precisely, even if enjoying himself, he would race back home from wherever he was. He was a man on a mission. His foot went hard down on the accelerator pedal, one hand gripped the steering wheel and the other wrestled with the gearbox, while the veins on his neck and face bulged alarmingly as his high blood pressure rose still further up the scale. For what? So he could take his siesta. An ironical and sad tale on reflection.

Life is a carousel and we find ourselves riding the same horse and coming back to the same situation. But then maybe, the ultimate happens. We lose our grip on the merry-go-round of neurotic reality.

*

Here, too, we come full circle, back to the subject of finding our self through madness. In losing the stays of our adaptations, we are grabbed by forces which swing us round like a dervish. Psychic patterns fragment into myriad shapes which disappear into the ether or become absolutes.

When I felt that I had 'lost my marbles', I counted the days of the week between therapy sessions like beads strung out on an abacus. The slightest alteration to my appointment time felt like the end of the world was nigh. This primal state seemed everlasting. If this regular contact was in jeopardy, so was I. My pre-programmed form having been smashed into smithereens, all I had now was my crazy world to hold onto. I could but hang in there.

But at long last, what should have been instilled into me as a child started to sink in - that amongst this chaos I had all the right building materials for my new foundations. Essentially it was a do-it-yourself job of assiduously collecting my disparate impulses together. After much turning and twisting, the wonder came when I saw these falling into place and a natural order of symmetrical patterns, as in a kaleidoscope.

Although still reliant on some reasonably constant factors around me, I no longer feel in such disarray when the unexpected happens. No more is my therapist my core point of reference. The pendulum of life seems to swing more from a pivotal centre within my body, the initial significator as to what truly serves us in the moment. We will, therefore, make some biopsychological links here.

* ✱ *

Section B   Ongoing mind-body patterns

Our body 'in-forms' our psyche and our psyche has an investment in our body. Particularly in infancy, we are bombarded with stimuli and we will desperately try to form a manageable pattern out of the confusion. More brain connections are laid down in the first year of life than at any future time. These can be hard to change.

Sometimes, there is little conscious communication between psyche and soma. If, when little, we split off from our instinctual self because it felt unsafe for this to become evident, although our psychic connections are shut down, the residue of many repressed sensory and emotional memories – genetic, collective and personal – will be left in our body. Since this way of subduing emotions generally becomes a habitual response, the areas holding these psychic imprints may lose full sensibility.

It follows that as our primary wound accumulates more layers of trapped emotions and these condense into armoured patterns of distress, so can the body's fascia eventually atrophy. For instance, hardening our heart may make us more susceptible to having a coronary. Poor physical health can be a symptom of deeply buried feelings since memory is distributed throughout the nervous system.

Physical 'dis-ease' is usually considered more acceptable than psychological disorder and more readily affords us sympathy and support. We tend to feel a legitimate right to receive the care and attention which, deep down, our psychically wounded self longs for. This may encourage us to deflect painful, seemingly hazardous, drives and emotions through somatic disorder.

Some manipulate others this way. The proverbial headache which forestalls sexual and/or verbal intercourse can be manifest through tensing up our neck and shoulders in order to hold in hostile feelings. With no emotional outlet, over time, chronic tension builds so that our body may devise even cleverer ways of shutting down. I had a patient who suffered from both *tinnitus* and *vaginismus*, until she was able to say 'shut up' to her vociferous husband.

Sometimes we learn to be stoic around physical pain. How about you? Are you big and brave when ill, or do you take to your bed at the first sign of a sneeze and expect to be waited on?

When I was three years old my mother took me to the doctor's surgery because I had lost my appetite. Now I suspect that this was symptomatic of having received an overdose of verbal abuse. But while I had tried to block this out, together with the painful and angry effects, it had manifested as an inflamed inner ear which had become impacted and burst. Apparently, the doctor was amazed that I had not complained of feeling any pain as this must have been considerable. But why would I? I was conditioned to suffer in silence.

We also safeguard ourselves from intolerable and inadmissible emotional hurt by contorting our body into shapes which become fixed and we suffer physical pain instead. A quick look in the mirror says it all. We might slump with the heaviness of our feelings or protect our vulnerable heart so get round shoulders. Alternatively we puff out our chest as we take on the world and then the base of our spine suffers with the weight of it all. The list of psychological equivalents to anatomical deformations is long.

*

Unless we are in touch with sensory impressions at the moment of impact, we will not be fully aware of our feeling response to a situation. For example, the effect of fear, and its sibling excitement, causes many somatic changes. The heart beats faster, blood vessels to the brain and fight and flight muscles, open wider. But do we notice our heart pumping away sixty to the dozen and fluttery sensations in our solar plexus as nerves fire-off their impulses? If we do recognise these promptings, do we attend to our emotional and physical well being or do we automatically tighten our midriff and inhibit our breathing?

Also, to free up extra supplies of energy for lifesaving activity, our digestive system shuts down so that our mouth becomes dry and our stomach clenches. If these early warning signs are ignored, any provocative talk at the dining table, for instance, could trigger a dose of indigestion. When we do not respond effectively to this secondary distress signal, digestive discomfort might develop into a hiatus hernia or chronic bowel disorder.

Physical constriction, inflammation and irritation may be somatic conversions of latent fear, hate and anger which generally, in turn, covers the pain of not having our needs met. With indigestion, say, it might be that expressing our feelings could bring greater relief than an antacid pill. Better to know when our integrity is under threat, if we are emotionally undernourished or overloaded. Indeed, the common complaint that we may be 'going down with a bout of something', might well mean an unconscious emotion is fighting to come up.

If we cannot transform the charge of energy activated by emotional factors, we become uptight or depressed. Of course we can always run to the gym. Physical activity, like relaxation techniques, both quietens and frees up emotional pressure - for a time. All the while, however, an ideal hotbed for psychosis may be simmering under the wraps of our adapted body self.

*

How we process and interpret present situations is conditioned by our past which so often plays havoc with present reality and our predictions of the future. Indeed, research studies indicate that how we are programmed to respond to stress as adults can be determined in the womb.

It is even argued that we arrive in this world with a backload of past life experiences. My hallucinations might indicate that I suffered violent deaths in previous incarnations, or that these illusions were in my biological system which sprang from my ancestors, with the result that my genetic chemistry predisposed me to be particularly sensitive. Either might be true - or not.

Furthermore, along with the charts of fate and astrology, there may be a correlation between our passage through life and the pattern of our birth. Using the *Birth Perinatal Matrix* as model, a reluctance to leave the womb, an entrapment or rushed propulsion through the birth canal, any forceps or drug intervention, are all identifiable influences which can parallel how we face the different stages in our psychic growth and move in general. Studies further show that how we latch onto our mother's breast indicates future attachments. Thus for some the land flows with milk and honey while for others, the world is a dangerous place.

Whether it is innate, perinatal or infantile programming that informs us as to how the land lies, if we do not establish a healthy mind-body connection when young, we will probably continue to stifle or misread our body's signals.

Of course, the issue of inheritance is a great ploy to explain away our difficulty in breaking fixated patterns - that this is just how we were made. Yet, to some extent, our innate chemical and emotional make-up will always have been modified by our primary carers. Certain characteristics were fostered and others inhibited.

Indeed, in our need for emotional sustenance, systems of control can be so drilled into our brain that, like Pavlov's dogs, we automatically respond in a particular way to a certain trigger. We see ourselves as victims of circumstance. We remain faithful to our introjected and projected masters and obey our basic programming like a computer. Rather than follow our true figuration, we maintain rigid bodily control, habits and belief constructs in order to give us some sense of continuity, attachment and cohesion.

While our way naturally follows our first, therefore deepest impressions, if we continually follow the tracks laid down for us, they may fracture under stress and we go off the rails. Where to now? So many moments of our lives are influenced by footprints from our past and taking footsteps into unknown territory can be daunting.

We all require some sequential structure on which to travel through life. This need for a sense of progression and of 'catching up with ourselves' is graphically portrayed in the book *Awakenings* (Sacks, 1973) which was later made into a film. Dr Sayer observed how his patients, newly released from their zombie state, stopped walking when they reached a particular area in the ward where there was a bare expanse of floor. Eventually, he came up with an idea. He had lines painted on this blank area and his patients were then able to move forward quite freely. With these guidelines they felt sufficiently safe to activate, exercise and register their advancement through time and space.

When our true self's natural development was originally arrested, we became frozen in that moment - real time stood still and our body and psyche stuck.

With *electro convulsive therapy* for the severely depressed, the cogs of the patient's time clock might be jerked into action so that the person starts functioning again but it is a mechanical adjustment to the brain's laid down pathways. Of course, such intervention has proved a life saver to many who seem lost to this world. It puts them out of their misery. But without them linking back to when their psyche-soma signals were initially interrupted, they may never apprehend who they really are.

When insulated from our genuine feelings and thoughts, we are essentially absent. It is like living in a hypnotic trance. Of course we will not know that until our core comes out of storage and we wake up to something different.

Two long term clients, with no apparent connection and at different times, used exactly the same words to express how they felt, quite spontaneously, 'as if nothing has been real in the past, that it is just a story'. I knew what they meant. Years previously, when I remembered what felt like my early demise, I had exclaimed 'My life is a lie'. It was as if I had been suspended in a weird psychic pool ever since. How I bless the person who then had said, 'This might be so, but now, you are in the present telling your truth'.

*

Compulsive body-mind practices divert attention away from trapped emotions. Before I went berserk emotionally I was a workaholic like my parents. I was a prime example of adhering to familial patterning. My home was a hive of activity and my social life a whirl and I would go through endless contortions to keep it that way.

Many of us run round like headless chickens, our psyche scrambled and cut off from our body. Anaesthetised to sensory impressions, we do not hear the alarm bell when it is time to stop and gather our self. It is somewhat a chicken and egg syndrome as to which comes first.

But unlike Humpty Dumpty, having broken my shell, I could put my self together. While some of my edges are still frayed, since I have a backlog of emotional injury to deal with, my psyche now resonates more easily with my body.

A few years ago my friend was registered as disabled. Having always fought courageously to 'keep going', despite suffering some harrowing life events, her considerable physical suffering distracts her from caring for her extreme emotional pain. It is her way.

Where sensory impressions remain encased and therefore not channelled through our psyche creatively, our body can become like a heaving rubbish dump. We become rotten at the core of our being when cut off from the deepest roots of our existence, as there is no life-giving flow of emotions filtering through. The affectation of lies which is buried festers and deforms.

Eating disorders and an excessive focus on body image are a cover up for not experiencing true power, worth and inner beauty. Whether addicted to work, daring pursuits, exercise, repetitive tasks, drink, drugs or sex, each demonstrates an attempt to alleviate the anxiety emanating from a repressed need and a precarious sense of self.

Another psychosomatic pattern is to harm our body directly. This is a drastic act but one which affords some momentary relief from unbearable body tension by bringing emotional pain to the surface. It also means that the suffering becomes visible to others. But more importantly, it will be self evident. This is because we are desperate for confirmation that our suffering is real if we learned to dissociate from painful feelings when young because no-one noticed us hurting. I would take this further and say that in feeling the physical pain we know that we are alive. Also, when we inflict violence on ourselves, we feel some sense of control. It is by our hand that we are hurt and not by another.

Self harm is difficult to witness and to understand therefore, often, it is dealt with harshly. But it is not uncommon for people to allow, or incite, another to physically hurt them and some 'accidents', as with illness, might well serve their purpose of externalising deeply buried psychic pain.

The deep primal wound never heals completely. We will always have a sore patch to look after. But I have found that it can diminish in size and the scar fade, if it is exposed in psychosis.

Some persistent maladjustments, including *phobias*, P.T.S.D. and addictions, to deeply-seated emotions may be interrupted or subdued by using mind-altering methods - from transcendental meditation, *E.M.D.R.* and hypnosis to *cognitive behavioural therapy* techniques and self improvement regimes. With such mediums, we can readjust the myths stemming from childhood around which our body-mind systems still operate. New problem solving skills, which challenge the validity of our early perception, may be learned so that signals of distress are received, reinterpreted and handled differently at an immediate level.

Moderating mind sets in order to allay the symptom, however, does not change the core issue, so I have found. This stays stored in the body, often only to reappear later in a different form. Transformation has to come from within. In treating symptoms behaviourally or with drugs, the opportunity to recognise what the suffering soul is trying to make explicit through the physical form can be lost. Symptoms are making a statement and have a purpose.

To cite a well known example - panic attacks occur when extreme somatic excitation rises up and, due to conditioning, anxiety is not channelled through normal outlets. Such attacks are disabling as the fear of having one can precipitate it happening. Anticipating a stressful situation automatically activates adrenaline and cortisol release. It is circular. What we expect we get.

With panic attacks the attention is on the situational trigger and the physical effect, rather than on the deeper emotional cause. While the subjective, overwhelming experience is of extreme powerlessness, this feeling covers the unconscious fear of raw and potentially destructive powerfulness. Many people with this disorder, and those who witness an attack, never find this out for themselves, so effective is this mechanism of repression.

Those who suffer this way often speak of feeling strangled. What is happening is that the pressure from repeatedly holding down emotions in their body has built up to such a degree and they are so terrified of their expulsion, that their chest and throat muscles automatically constrict.

Along with my psychotic episodes, I had many panic attacks and was sure I was about to expire. I would choke on my tongue as I tried to swallow back waves of forceful energy - a result of a suffocating childhood and physical sensations not being sufficiently mediated through mother in the *oral phase*.

*

Here we re-enter the fantastical realms in order to explore more subtle energy patterns, initially, through the medium of Alice in Wonderland. One interpretation of the Red Queen's cry, '*Off with her head!*' is that this indicates Alice's fear of reprisal by her mother when taking steps towards individuation. I once danced the role of Alice and this fear was transferred onto my ballet teacher. However, I also associate the Red Queen's command with how mad elements demand release – such is the tension between what is physically held below the neck and the mental functioning above.

It has been suggested that I have had a *rogue kundalini* experience. This is the name given to when the base chakra, deemed a centre for the primitive drives, is opened under extreme pressure. Under the tutelage of a master *shaman*, apparently, a pure kundalini release may be harnessed into an esoteric power which can be utilised for profound understanding and healing. However in my case, supercharged energetic forces shot up directly into the top chakra and became relatively divorced from my body. Without any processing through the intermediary chakras, the raw primal elements conjoined with the transpersonal elements and a conflict of Armageddon proportions resulted.

The word 'rogue' reminds me of a rampant elephant charging, which describes well how unstoppable these rushes of escaping forces felt. For a year or so afterwards, I could follow the precise direction of energy streams flowing along specific channels, called *meridians*, inside me. Not a pleasant feeling, but one which confirmed for me the theory that there are subtle energy pathways both through and around our form.

We all unconsciously pick up what people emanate to some extent. But an early warning radar system can become highly developed in a primary environment which exhibits no clear reliable messages. With only vague clues to rely on, we learn to intuit, through sensory perception, what is going on around us.

Being ultra sensitive might be a blessing. The ability to configure abstract sensory messages in the surrounding *field* into judicious information is useful, particularly for a therapist when a client's emotions are not fully conscious, and/or stem from infancy, so that verbal communication is difficult.

But such sensibility also can be a curse. It is easy to misinterpret what emanates from people who remind us of our primary carers. Furthermore, we may not realise that what we are feeling does not belong to us. We can become a psychic sponge if we habitually get under another's skin, so to speak, and merge - such might be our primal body's patterning.

Where the veil is gossamer fine, however, as in psychosis, we can take on free-floating energy completely or perceive that the other person has taken on ours. We can feel we are them and they us - strange but true. If the window is open to the paranormal realms what is beyond understanding happens.

*

A more normal and time-honoured practice of contacting what is not fully conscious is through dreams and nightmares. These can represent, give us again in different forms, an underlying concern and may help to dissolve its force for a while. They are a system of counterbalancing neurotic splitting. Indeed, under the cover of sleep, we may regress to the symbolic, archetypal and raw infantile drives which reign in the psychotic domain, yet remain safeguarded from the full sensory and psychic experience.

When I was facilitating a woman to enter more fully into a recurring nightmare, she relayed that she physically felt ligatures binding her legs. She later found out, from a family friend, that she was indeed restrained in this way as a child. When grounding this replay, she said with firm conviction, 'Now I know for sure that this truly happened. I will never doubt or forget the truth of this experience as I have felt it in my body.'

With this physical confirmation of what had haunted her since childhood, previously manifest in more unconscious ways such as panicking if a trouser or car seat belt felt tight, came a sense of release. Her nightmares and physical reaction to constraint might now quieten, and her memory find some place of rest in her psyche.

A dream can be of a wish fulfillment, a dread or what has happened that day or back in our past. Hallucinations can incorporate all these things and also stem from our instinctual primordial source. In such productions, imagination links with sensory apparatus to dramatise urges and ideals.

Likewise, memory can be a reconstruction of a scenario which attracts or 're-collects' latent, associated emotions from different episodes, times and memory banks or complexes. Thus, without a factual basis of an event having taken place, it should not be translated too literally. Even short term memory has been shown as unreliable.

False Memory Syndrome is a worrying and controversial subject. Believing a retrieved memory as correct in all its hard facts is dangerous; it can cause longstanding and widespread damage to all concerned. Furthermore, for a therapist to subtly instill, or foster, the idea of a particular repressed memory, is abusive in itself. However, for a therapist to hold the possibility that a memory stems from a wish in childhood, say for sexual gratification, alongside the fact that such abuse does occur, poses huge challenges.

Asking a client to accommodate the notion that such a memory might be fabricated, particularly when flashbacks seem so alive, will most likely be felt as further denial. Such a cruel replay can be devastating and might supercharge the chaotic emotions and sensations accompanying the memory. However, in time, out of a willingness to stay with this horrible conflict may develop real self respect and maybe, validation that the essence of the memory is true.

From ongoing clinical trials, Bowlby, the founder of primary attachment theory, spoke of children suffering trauma: *Evidence shows that many of these children, aware of how their parents feel, proceed then to conform to their parents' wishes by excluding from further processing such information as they already have; and that, having done so, they cease consciously to be aware that they have ever observed such scenes, formed such impressions, or had such experiences.* (Karen, R. 1994)

Post Traumatic Stress Disorder demonstrates how convoluted both memory and programmed reactions are. The external boundaries and internal membranes of the body and mind have been opened wide, due to a major assault, and have stayed that way. Thus there is no conscious filtering which enables recognition of what are real threats to survival and what stem from earlier trauma. The brain's chemical and neurological threads have forged such deep patterns that they are on a continual feedback loop. Emotional circuits have become 'hard wired', therefore they are in a constant state of hyper arousal. Permanently alert to presumed danger, in this tangled neuron net, terror takes on a life of its own.

I remember how the slightest of triggers could throw me back to incidents when I was terrified as a youngster. I experienced these blasts from the past as if they were happening all over again in the present. Such is the power of the body to store every detail that it can recreate all sensory and emotional perceptions. Expressing these had been forbidden as a child and the traumas were so forbidding that I had had to wipe them out. I had many flashbacks when I was petrified, stuck as if the film was freeze-framed, and it has taken years for the memories to free up so I could move on.

To mitigate the full horror of intolerable trauma we create dissociative defences by separating the effects of the experience from the meaning. This point of splitting I found to be the crux of the matter of madness. Therefore in a more sane and balanced time, I knew that I must recover the part of me that had remained encased in this impasse; the child caught in this hellish state of betwixt and between for decades who witnessed being violated from above and did not dare come back down into the physical experience.

Eventually, I found that I could manage to hold myself together sufficiently to regress voluntarily to what I had relived so vividly in flashbacks, and I came to the point where I could not deny what had happened to me any longer. I knew that this abuse was true but that I could not handle the sensations and emotions engendered at the actual time. I was so young then. I had neither the outside support nor sufficient internal reasoning to process it.

Generally, a deeply repressed memory only surfaces when defensive structures are shaken up sufficiently for trapped cellular feeling states to discharge their energy. While facts are often distorted, the emotion which arises in a memory from our unconscious, particularly when it reverberates in the body, is real and it needs acknowledging as a source of pertinent reclamation of our true self - we feel it 'in our bones'. When we continue to repeat and re-enact intense experiences, it means that they hold a fundamental principle which we need to deal with.

Holding emotions in our body is exhausting as well as being detrimental to our physical and psychological health. An example of short term memory retrieval is of a woman, suffering whiplash from a car accident, who was referred to me because no amount of osteopathic treatment had managed to release her neck trauma. When I encouraged this patient to record the accident during a massage however, she began to give vent to the anger she felt towards the driver responsible. As if by magic, her spine clicked into place. In freeing her emotions, she could release the tension in her neck. The physical evidence was no longer needed.

Some words about catharsis here. It can feel good to scream and sob as our body may be relieved of tension for a while. However, such release can become an obsessional and addictive pattern in itself. Particularly if flooded by sensations which have no meaning, periods must follow when connection to a mediating other is sought. By these means, mental constructs may form around such disparate forces.

*

Our body contains the blueprint which affords great potential for expansion. Along with the impulse to embody soul, enter matter and be born, a basic instinct is to suckle from the breast. Thus we reach out for our mother or substitute, in order to come into relationship with her and through her, to our self - from genetic to systematic programming.

If, as a youngster, we were able to relax so that sensory impressions gradually integrated with psychic connections to become experienced feeling states, we will have a flexible psyche-soma container. There is no substitute for having internalised being held safely by loving arms when little.

Where this is not the case, however, we might return to our primal material and find such holding within the therapeutic space - which future chapters will go into. Primal needs cannot be satisfied from outside as the infant years will not come again. But without connecting back to this time in adulthood, our body and mind may not clearly communicate with each other.

The best chance to counterbalance any faulty mind sets instilled in us, is to listen to what our body is trying to tell us. All the neurotic patterning of the adapted self, the body armour and the configurations from the psychotic layer, are formations which protect us from the terrible state where there is no continuing sense of being. Yet our senses leave numerous tender trails for us to follow which lead back home to our emotional being.

From this elemental place, we may recuperate substantial vigour. Bizarre as it may seem, through the muck and muddle of psychosis we might ultimately come into harmony with our self and with the fundamental principles in the wider world. Thereby we gain both physical and psychological health.

Whether it was the fickle hand of fate, random choice or deterministic principle arising from my nature and nurturing which prompted me to take this particular fork in my journey, I cannot say for sure. But I do know that my early set patterns have radically changed since rallying to the protest coming from my body tissues.

Whatever the form, whether an arousing call to sojourn to our true being comes as a psychotic or a spiritual emergence, what precedes can be felt through sensory impressions. Parched of wholesome outlets, our body can feel tense, drained and dispirited. We have reached the point when we are able to withstand no longer the restrictions of our lifelong format. Something has to give and it surely does when elementary or transpersonal elements burst forth. We are then compelled to take cognisance of what our body is trying to tell us. The tinkling bell that once rang from our oscillating emotional body which we ignored, now reverberates as a siren. It has become a clarion wake-up call.

In ancient mythology, when the seeds of earth, sea and sky were considered to slumber in a confused and shapeless mass, the period was called Chaos. Out of the mindlessness and mystery of psychosis, a true connection might flow between our body, feeling, mind and spiritual layers. By losing our mind, and with it our patterned adaptations, our life-force gradually enters hitherto deadened places so that we may take possession of our fuller self.

On this journey of discovery there are no direct learning curves, rather we spiral around many times in our psychological growth. Similarly, this chapter started along the lines of repeating childhood patterns, only to end with finding a new order out of chaos. We will now explore this circle in a wider context.

✷

Chapter 6

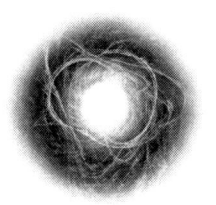

A Perspective of Madness and Sanity

Section A   Symptoms and defences, procedures and attitudes

What is this thing called madness? While humans have evolved so that instincts have become secondary, these still can be held in the *brain stem* which dates back to man's evolution from reptiles. Unless integrated and refined sufficiently, these primitive drives may become so forceful that they override higher structures of cortex reasoning. When these combine with subsequently suppressed sensory and emotional states, the person can be thrown into psychosis.

A stereotypical image is of an unkempt creature with wild eyes who is ranging around uttering profanities. Another version is that of a totally inert soul, a sorry specimen curled up in a corner. But when not in extremis, since psychotic elements are part of human nature, there is no definitive, reassuring dividing line between mental health and illness – yet how earnestly we try to draw one.

Most of us will have experienced, for a short time and in a reduced form, some of the symptoms of psychosis which appear in the Diagnostic and Statistical Manual (The American Psychiatric Association, 1994). This is not to suggest that we have been classified as insane, or that we may, or need to, become so. The way towards true self emergence for the deeply wounded might mean a close shave with madness but most certainly is not through becoming defined by it.

Thus here, as well as looking at psychiatric illnesses and how they are, and might be, treated, in Section B more moderate disorders will be illustrated. Comparisons will be made between neurotic and psychotic symptoms and also between narcissistic and *borderline* traits. In Section C some of the foregoing is taken into a social and global perspective where the emphasis is on how we might come to our true senses.

While primitive energies are common to all, because our genesis is individual the ways in which these emerge in psychosis are manifold and idiosyncratic. Therefore, while some aspects of my story will resonate with people who know what a touch of madness feels like, there will be those who have had quite different experiences. Yet, whatever the difference in form or severity, a sense of being inwardly empty seems to be primary in all psychic disorder.

For instance, clinical *unipolar depression* is marked with feelings of hopelessness, helplessness, unworthiness and of not having a legitimate place in the world. Nothing has any meaning to a severe depressive. Lethargy, or agitation, and apprehension can take hold so there is withdrawal from others, which furthers the sense of non existence. Naturally, buried under the blanket of depression is a vast reservoir of energy from the dynamic primal forces, particularly anger. But the depressives' unconscious fear is that if such archaic libido were released, their fragile self would be overwhelmed.

Mania lies at the other end of the pole. As in primary narcissism, manic people re-experience the feeling that the world revolves around them and that they can rule, save and destroy it. Mania is generally a reactive defence against deflation, aloneness and terror of non being. Therefore, when sufferers eventually realise that people around them are not supporting their inflated sense of self, there is nothing left for them but to tumble down into empty depression again. People who swing from these high and low polarities are diagnosed as having bipolar affective disorder, once called manic depression. There is little middle ground between these cycles.

A patient would bowl into my treatment room one week full of 'joie de vivre', throwing out spectacular plans to expand his business and scale new heights in dangerous sports - nothing could stop him - only to limp in a month later in utter despair. He could not be bothered, the future was bleak and life was not worth living - until the next manic flight.

Paranoia is when everything has a special meaning and there is a continual threat in the atmosphere. This beset me for a while and the overarching danger in many psychopathological conditions is that paranoia can lead to the most serious mental illness, schizophrenia. People with schizophrenia may have periods of remission when they operate quite normally. But when ill, they withdraw *'from people and reality, often into a fantasy life of delusions and hallucinations'* (Davison and Neale, 1998) where they have practically no sense of who they are.

*

Mental health procedures can either inhibit or help developing a core sense of self.

Gone are the years of lunatic asylums when whips were used to drive out the vile forces of the damned inmates. For this we can thank the Freudian, Jungian and Adlerian practices which entered mental institutions around World War 1. However, they were quickly overtaken by innovative physical treatments as psychiatry melded with mainstream medical practice. These included the administration of poorly researched mind-altering drugs and both chemical and electrical convulsions, as well as the surgical procedure of leucotomy where certain tracts of the frontal lobes are destroyed. From such fearsome experiments emerged modern day treatments which have been so refined that they greatly relieve the suffering of the mentally disturbed and are far less troublesome and time consuming than therapy.

Whether you approve of such aids or not, restrictive legislation, strait jackets, padded cells, white coats, drugs and more extreme, some subtle, physical and psychic interventions, all may give much sought-after restraining and supportive structures to those experiencing severe mental disturbance.

Likewise, when someone is placed in a particular category of mental illness, this can create a sense of control and containment. For the practitioner, it provides a prognosis and an objective framework to proceed with. For the patient, being identified with a particular condition may afford relief in that their symptoms are recognisable and so might be curable. There is an official language and common ground to work on.

With this greater organisation however, there are drawbacks. Differences can be overlooked in order to fit someone's profile into a particular category. Moreover, diagnosis and prescriptive treatment can stop two-way original and soulful thinking and feeling. Creativity gets boxed in when the manifestation of a disordered psyche becomes the definition of who the sufferer is.

While diagnostic labels for the psychically disturbed are politically correct, they can desensitise society. More particularly, they can dehumanise those with mental problems by further stripping them of dignity and of what limited sense they have of selfhood. Care and knowledge of self is taken over by the practitioner.

So much in my experience signifies that, although we have learnt a lot over the last century about the treatment of psychosis, another radical change is due. My reasoning is that underlying most grievances in general medical practice, from staff and patients, is the primal need to be seen and heard. Yet while cognition of the links between mind, body and soul increases, the attitude that gives rise to trying to banish psychotic forces remains. This paradox is swelling the demand for both therapy and palliative care. But having placed such reliance on diagnosis and scientific medical procedures, the emotional and financial resources of the public mental health services are strained almost to breaking point.

My hope is that more natural ways of healing the mind will satisfy this demand in the same way as more food is being produced organically and sourced locally. Despite all our modern sophistication, common sense is now drawing us 'back to basics'. So might attention be directed towards the original source of mental disorder. This may prove more cost effective and manageable, more succinct and productive, than when energy is spread over its diverse symptoms. Investment in mental health might show greater and longer lasting dividends if channelled towards what is at the heart of the matter.

For many, this primary need used to be assuaged by a spiritual conviction that, through sacrifice of self, we would be rewarded in heaven. Now, for the most part, no longer does a religious community provide a sense of identity. Furthermore, modern day technology alienates us from Mother Nature, our collective holding source, which once connected us to our instinctual roots and our fellowmen. Sometimes, all we are left with is our feelings of being adrift and incomplete.

How can this absolute need be met? In the first place, if the root cause of mental disorder - that is the lack of evidential true self - can be held foremost in the minds of mental health practitioners while classifying and treating symptoms, a space opens for those impaired to expand into - one where the presence of self may be revealed.

Of course, there is no guarantee, however resourceful the treatment, because with congenital or subsequent chronic neural or chemical disorder, or for those who suffered extreme assaults in childhood, the life-line may be irreparable. But that is not to say that we should give up trying since some recognition may filter through. Indeed, a higher than average proportion of Romanian babies, those who were left in orphanages without any chance of emotional engagement, were assessed as autistic. Their feeling self seemed unreachable. Yet, where deep respect and love was subsequently available to them, it was shown to have good effect.

For the core self to flourish, however, communication of a more concrete kind is also essential. Here we have a big stumbling block. For a practitioner to encourage his patient to verbalise psychotic material or to act this out while he, the practitioner, remains fully present, generally is thought only to fan the fire. Such an idea leads into dangerous territory where both parties might lose all sanity (Laing, 1959). Therefore, pathological energies are usually quenched with medication despite this form of expression often being the only way that those with 'unsound' mind can relate to another human being.

I hasten to add here that, for some individuals, drugs are a necessity and that the only feasible treatment is to help them live with mental disturbance by strengthening their survival strategies. Not everyone with a mental condition has sufficient resources to go through the rigours of deep therapy.

I would encourage such people to take their medication and, particularly those who find bouts of mania so seductively intoxicating, to read *The Unquiet Mind* by Kay Redfield Jamison (1996) who, as a Professor of Psychiatry and a manic depressive herself, really knows what she is writing about. She is also a staunch supporter of patients being able to help heal themselves with talking therapy. The ideal must be to draw from both. Without such concomitant work, there are no pathways for integrating the symptoms. Instead, these can be put down to merely biological dysfunction.

Anti-psychotic drugs are a quick and easy means of stabilising an excitable or distressed patient. Therefore they are often given as a 'first aid' in crisis management. However, while medication may be effective in the short term, it will often need to continue in order to prevent the risk of periodic relapse. The acute turns into a chronic condition, albeit contained.

Psychotic elements are not foreign bodies. Instead of attacking them with drugs as if they were invading toxins, our system may reconstitute this essential matter by assimilating and refining what is rightfully ours. Drugs do not cure the fundamental problem. They might blunt the pain and help us to function in the normal world. But they immobilise the very constituents which may bring us inner strength. In quietening such excitation, palliative remedies might also reduce the motivational impulse of soul wanting to manifest. They stem the life flow. Our survivor aspect is empowered, while our core substance is disempowered.

I believe that everyone has the right to know these facts and to be offered extensive talking therapy. But unless we understand the rudiments of this process before we fall into the throes of a psychotic breakdown, chances are this decision will be made for us by authoritative professionals; whereas aided by such information, we might more fully enter into choosing and engaging in our particular form of treatment. Knowing the potential pitfalls and perks, we can decide to attempt a journey through psychosis towards wholeness, or settle on a compromising cure.

Innumerable people before me have recognised that the underlying source of much mental disturbance lies in the early formative years. But I would go further. For some of us whose wounds run deep, developing a really robust inner strength might only come through regressing to the time and state when our authentic self felt wiped out. Fear of a mental breakdown, generally buried deeply in all of us, and, more importantly for the severely primally wounded, the possibility of going mad, may persist unless worked through.

My suggestion that more of us voluntarily take this hazardous route may well seem crazy to many. Not wishing to polarise but to bring us into a more balanced whole, I would further propose that a society which accepts, even encourages, an obsession with work, materialism and hedonistic pleasures is equally crazy. The symptomatic desire for a constant fix to lift our mood is a neurotic attempt to alleviate the pain of self abandonment, which feels too awful to attend to.

*

So who is going to help give psychosis the creative place it deserves?

One reason for my strongly delivered message as to the potential curative effect of psychosis is to help shake up the entrenched view of what is true mental health. I consider that prospect well worth any backlash I might get from questioning therapeutic practices and from my exposition of personal madness.

Whatever else this rendition brings, some therapists may be encouraged to explore further the psychotic domain. Others might only dispel it but with the question remaining as to whether those with deep pathology seeking their help would be better off working with someone who has grown through psychosis. Being open to uncertainty can still work wonders.

Mental disorder, by nature, is full of conundrums. Moreover, its contradictions and anomalies, which inhibit the sufferers' ability to be coherent and cohesive, can affect and be reflected in the psyche of practitioners. This lack of integration runs throughout the background and practice of depth psychology. The splitting which is fundamental in all forms of mental illness exists in the profession which serves to both diagnose and treat it. While the need for deep and true connection is universal, it is particularly vital in the mental health profession.

It is fitting to say that most analytical and therapeutic schools welcome the emergence of a client's elementary material, to some degree. Lying on a *psychoanalyst*'s couch is likely to induce deep regression. Yet, as in the training analysis of an analyst and the personal therapy of a psychotherapist, generally a mental breakdown is frowned upon – it is deemed a failure by professional bodies just as society would judge it to be.

I believe, however, that the foundations of such establishments would be all the stronger if a skirmish with madness was considered healthy preparation for working in the field of mental health. Rather than be an indicator of fragility, the demanding process ultimately invigorates. It is a plausible starting point.

As it is, people who work in the front line with severely disturbed patients, those who give day to day care, often have minimal personal therapy, training and support. Sadly, although dedicated to their vocation and doing much good and loving work, many practitioners only survive because they are expert at dissociating. Furthermore, some who have undergone more long term therapy, particularly therapists who major in proactive techniques, I have experienced as having a strongly developed adapted self which closely borders the inflated narcissist's false self.

I have been in different trainings where the exposure and challenge of shadow elements was sincerely encouraged. But the benefits of practitioners journeying into their psychotic layer, of making room for the possibility of entering madness in their personal therapy, was never emphasised sufficiently, in my opinion. Therefore, there is a dearth of therapists who have themselves been to the pit of the psyche and who have stayed long enough to find their fulsome reality and sanity.

Most clinical teaching affords a sound basis of

understanding and treating psychosis, along with a firm grasp of personal experience for practicing the art of healing *neurosis*. But the profound sensibility which may come from therapists working through psychosis can never be learnt in any professional training or clinical practice. It is not just their overt attitude. The subtle energies which therapists emit are even more pervasive and psychotic elements can easily hide behind a well 'therapised' psyche.

Even with the current tightening of training standards and the proliferation of therapists, of the many I have met, less than a handful have come through psychotic episodes without using pharmaceutical armaments, panaceas and/or sublimating therapy. The training for psychotherapists and analysts is generally long and arduous. Nevertheless, more of my colleagues might consider whether they owe it to themselves and to their profession to be fully shaken in these realms, then the experience can be used in the service of their clients.

Like Theseus (Grant & Hazel, 1973) and the Minotaur (an elemental being), a person who has journeyed into the psychotic realm, and returned, can extend a thread of hope to fellow travellers. However tenuous this contact, he can be the keeper of the gate which opens between the two worlds, so that, with patient attendance, other valiant souls might eventually find their way out of the labyrinth of madness.

※

The trammelled and tortured mind needs hope. When all the terrifying but rich qualities in Pandora's (*Ibid*) box have escaped, hope remains, although fragile and obscure. I have been inspired by Watts' (1886) portrayal of 'Hope' as a woman, who is blindfolded, sitting on the perimeter of the globe of the world. She clutches a lyre close to her ear and she is plucking its only string in the hope, perhaps, of hearing a note which resonates with her and other faint hearted souls.

Sadly, the mentally disturbed are out of reach to most so-called normal people; their heartstrings do not strike an acceptable chord. Many suffer, holding only a flicker of faith that their sound will be heard by someone who can stay with them, while they wait for their true full voice to emerge.

Most of us have felt pain, fear and grief. Thus we can empathise with others to some extent, even if their degree of distress is horrific and way beyond our experience and therefore our full grasp. But madness is a cacophony of urges, emotions, sensations and images with which some might become familiar through observation and so can diagnose the cause, type and treatment, but few have had first hand experience.

An analyst who spoke about her psychoses from over forty years ago, writes:

Any person who is willing to bear frenzy, temporarily, to the point of losing his sense of identity and certainty of survival - in other words to 'break down', or reach chaos or catastrophe (the point of tension where he has to bear not being able to bear it) - will emerge from it with heightened abilities... It does not follow, of course, that everyone has to break down, or "go mad". (Little, 1981)

'Only the wounded healer heals' (Jung, 1946) is a fundamental premise. Indeed, the more wounds a therapist has, the greater the potential benefit to his client, if these wounds are being attended to. 'It takes one to know one,' so the saying goes. Of course, we can never know another fully, even though our primal needs are much the same. We are unique and so is our pathology. We are, however, more able to comprehend and attune with psychotically disturbed souls, when we have felt the throes of madness ourselves. Such people are sorely needed.

No one can process all their psychopathology in a lifetime. Some personal elements, therefore, will always remain in a therapist's unconscious and these will inevitably affect the client, however many supervisory sessions a therapist takes regarding the client. Accordingly, it is the responsibility of those who offer in-depth psychological support to commit to intensive and ongoing personal therapy. I advocate that this should be mandatory for all but exceptionally mature therapists.

I am not suggesting that current mental health policy be axed, rather that more practitioners work through their own psychoses and their help be phased in. Certainly, such a commitment will mean a lot of soul searching and support.

But, rather than make even more unreasonable demands on the public and private mental health sectors, the profoundly enriched energy from the practitioners' unconscious, can be ploughed back into the profession thus increasing the available 'man power' and long term monetary saving.

While I respect the challenging and sterling work which professionals do, often with little reward, I am inspired to champion my view on the essential need of those who suffer from mental ill-health; people who live in unimaginable terror; who feel condemned to a life which is emotionally and spiritually impoverished; those whose existence feels so fragile and/or unmanageable; the many whose sanity depends on palliative care. All those who know what madness is like long to meet a person who has some personal understanding.

While mental health organisations, public and private, are awash with fine Mission Statements as to their direction and training, always the bottom line in my testimonial is to continue working towards knowing what lies at the base of the psyche - so our exploration continues.

※

Section B
Recognising our psychic disorders and defence mechanisms

Here, the objective is to bring psychological theory to life - your life. Imagine waking up to a world in an adult's body but with the limited and disorganised faculties of a baby. This is not to say that an infant has exactly the same experience as someone undergoing a psychotic episode. An infant has the freshness of instinct and receptivity, as well as the plasticity, to help him progress through the stages of growth. Normally, he is relatively cocooned from the rigours of the world, therefore, rather than be subsumed by archaic energies, there may be greater space and support for their organisation.

Other comparisons in psychic activity are important to understand. To start with, psychotic energies tend to be raw and primitive, whereas neurotic symptoms might be traced to a later stage of childhood development when there are more sophisticated defence mechanisms in place. These more surface symptoms demonstrate our 'wants' and are a reaction formation to placate our deeper, basic emotional and instinctual unmet 'needs'.

It follows that a neurotic response is due to a disturbance of a part of the adapted personality and comes from the fear of persecution, whereas a psychotic reaction arises from the terror of annihilation of the whole being. The neurotic person distorts reality whereas the psychotic gives it up.

To illustrate this difference, we can return to the example of the client who kept smiling although burdened by his family's sadness and high expectations. This man was searching for a fulfilling career but he found decision making difficult. What would others say about his choice and could he succeed? He was a perfectionist and he wanted to please everyone. No matter how hard he tried, nothing was ever enough; a view held by his parents, no doubt, but now by his internalised taskmaster.

He could not make up his own mind, it having been formed by others. Moreover, any encouragement towards, or indeed praise for, taking self responsibility was interpreted as a demand. He felt persecuted. There was nothing for it, he could only take on a *passive aggressive* stance - a neurotic defence against fear of failure and exposure of his unacceptable self.

When his exacting superego really got to him, he would move to the psychotic level when reality is abandoned. His entire thinking, feeling and behaviour were called into question. Could he trust his own mind or was it implanted by others? He, no longer, just doubted his judgment; he felt tormented and that people were out to destroy him completely. He relentlessly ran himself down. He thought that he was good for nothing, without value and not fit to live, let alone to determine his will. He was nothing. This man had realised his own self destruction. Having crashed through his neurotic barrier of fear, anger and shame, he had reached his psychotic terror of non being.

At a neurotic level he wanted praise from others. But getting what we want brings only transitory pleasure, whereas satisfying a need is life affirming and brings us closer to genuine happiness. His deepest need was to connect to what he truly felt and thought. He needed a sure feeling of self - the linchpin to good mental health.

Remarkably, our once total identification with our primary carers can remain at a psychotic level, even if we have ostensibly separated from them. Thus until the awful, mindless terror of annihilation is attended to, in certain circumstances no objective principle is available to us.

On the other hand, I know a youth who, despite a traumatic loss as a young child, is flourishing in the world. Having survived a car crash in which his parents died, he lived in an orphanage. Naturally, at first, he feared for his survival. But then he grieved, having had parents who nurtured his feeling self as a baby. His secure primary attachment has provided him with a strong root system through which he continues to be nourished, from within and without.

Not all survivors of horrific events, even those considered *'beyond the realms of normal human experience'* (Davison and Neale, 1998), suffer from Post Traumatic Stress Disorder. Neither do they dissociate from such events so that a part of them operates in a *schizoid* way, that is cut off from the resultant emotional effects. Many soldiers came out of Vietnam relatively unscathed. However, nearly one fifth were permanently terrorised because exposure to danger, physical and emotional, can have a long lasting effect when coupled with a residual terror of self annihilation.

From clinical experiments, some theorists believe that we arrive in this world already with some sense of self and that we can then lose this connection through primal wounding. Others consider that, before conception, during incubation and for a month after birth, there is no real sense of core being.

In some way, I feel that I have returned close to this state on quite a few occasions. It might have been only for a moment but nothingness seems endless. Naturally, this concept of non being is impossible to fully understand as we are tapping a pre-verbal time and also, if absolute, there would be no consciousness of not being present. Madness is full of imponderables. But in my experience, the terror of coming close to what is totally unknown, a lack of self in the void, is the nub of psychopathology.

The phrase 'frozen in fear' describes well how my brain sometimes seemed to fuse and I lost contact with any cerebral functioning. Now that is terrifying. I was in the rift between two minds where I stayed inert and paralysed. My febrile mind, having turned on me, then deserted me. My brain screamed silently but could make no connections, pictures or words. If only in minutiae, I felt what it might be like to be catatonic and totally cut off from self and others.

The following mantra is to encourage someone who is reliving the distress of hitherto repressed abuse: *'The pain that I might feel by remembering can't be any worse than the pain I feel by knowing and not remembering'*. Maybe at the neurotic level this is true. However, I have found that recovering the feelings from the deepest wounding to the emotional self, namely the abandonment of our core self, is more terrible than the suffering which accompanies any alternative deadening or self destructive procedures - hence their attraction.

Suicide is a radical, concrete re-enactment of this collapse into nothingness. Terrible as it might be, it may feel better to throw away a life that is not ours and one we feel contempt for, than remain living out a charade. Whether we are driven to kill ourselves in this dramatic way, opt to drag out our death by taking narcotics or to dull our primal pain through other life depleting ways, such symbolic actions show how unimaginable and unbearable the deep abject terror of non being is. Nothing, I repeat, nothing is as dreadful as this.

✱

Most of us make frantic efforts to fill the void and to relate through the neurotic devices of our adapted self. We can overdose on extraneous things, however, so much so that there is no space to build on what is truly important – our self. Of course we want to live life to the full, to feel important and fulfilled. But often, we are so neglectful of our inner world that we still feel at a loss.

We have many mechanisms for diverting attention away

from our primal needs and emotions which keep niggling away deep inside. Here are some already referred to which you might recognise:

Dissociation – splitting off a group of mental processes from consciousness
Distortion – experiencing delusional superiority
Idealisation/Devaluation – of carer/therapist rather than owning real feelings
Identification – assuming characteristics of another
Intellectualization – focussing on the illness not the person
Passive aggression – feigning tiredness to forestall sexual advancement
Rationalisation – using scientific explanation of the mystical
Reaction formation – attraction to opposite of what parents approve
Retroflection – self harm
Somatisation – panic attacks
Splitting self/others – making parents right, child wrong
Undoing – compulsive rituals

Emotions which stem from other situations, often from early beginnings, are also displaced onto others. There is the scenario of father returning home from a day at work, feeling humiliated by the boss who took him to task, who then takes it out on his wife. His wife turns on the eldest child who goes for his younger sister who kicks the cat. Chances are that this man was bullied by his father. But often we are so split off from the foundation of our distress that we have no idea as to why we reacted so strongly. While our need may be for compassion, to be comforted and loved, this need makes us vulnerable as it comes from a small, tender part in us. Thus our want and neurotic defence is to feel big and tough and so we act it out.

Many of us use people as objects and, sometimes material possessions take the place of people to help placate the disquiet that an emptiness deep inside brings.

Alternatively, some of us may strive to perpetuate the rapture of boundlessness and of being part of something bigger than ourselves as in maternal unity. In our heroic pursuit of the sacred and to escape from the horror and pain which absence of self brings, we stay skimming above our dense physical world. But the inner hunger to fill the void, wherein lies our undeveloped identity, is insatiable and can never be assuaged with such higher sidetracking. Rather than fully enter into matter and mortal relationships, contend with antagonistic forces of light and dark, we stay split off from our unwanted neurotic and psychotic elements. We project them onto others to carry and act out for us.

A few, however, go to the extreme and such pathology of the sublime, or stoic optimism, composure, anger or quiet depression can no longer be maintained. The outer coverings are divested and replaced by the awful protective mechanism of absolute denial which is full-scale psychosis. Everything is turned inside out to the extent that we totally split off our unruly projections and they act as attachment objects 'out there'.

When entrenched in the psychotic position, we have left the field of normal human interaction and we stay unconsciously fixated in the earliest phase of development when others seem unreal. Since normal society cannot reach the psychotic's reality, such a collapse could be deemed to be the deepest defence against making genuine relationships. We have reached the last bastion of defence against the ineffable state of non being.

It is telling that the temptation to stay on the planet of psychosis may be strongest when we are in this isolated place and, correspondingly, bordering the very core of our existence. I wish that everyone knew this.

*

I was angry with my friend; I told my wrath, my wrath did end. (Blake, 1992) Some have found that there is a better chance of recovery for psychotic individuals who express their hostility, than for those who stay resigned and submissive. Since hate is a hardened and constant version of anger, a frozen aggression without the flame of action, it needs deconstructing in order to develop and preserve selfhood. Self hatred will dissolve when we begin to accept and look after our elemental substance.

Where there is neither love nor hate, there is apathy. If

both these antagonistic emotions are shut down with indifference, there is little libido and a totally passive attitude to life. When such forces are walled in or heavily sedated, such is the being's inner emptiness that it appears as though a living corpse is walking through the world. The mumbling and ranting of the mad are a sign of not being able to assert their inherent power.

Referring again to the book, *Awakenings* (Sacks, 1973), Dr Sayer's experiments with the drug Dopamine in 1969 brought *post-encephalitis lethargica* patients out of their catatonic sleep. The initial response was for his patients to exhibit sober behaviour and these lost souls were then greeted enthusiastically by family, friends and the medical world. However, this approval of his treatment was short-lived as powerful base emotions, including rage and sexual urges, soon erupted from these patients.

What in my view was a healthy demonstration of invigorating primary energies were considered by medical authorities 'too hot to handle' and body spasms took over the patients which were further immobilised by drugs. Once again, disempowered, each returned to catatonia. Dr. Sayer subsequently declared to academics that '*the human spirit was more powerful than any drug*' - a wise and humble conclusion for a neurologist to make ... the jury is out.

While containment is vital in psychosis, this need for protection is generally viewed from a physical perspective. What is overlooked is the subconscious fear that madness is contagious and that we risk being drawn into the same orbit; that patches of paranoia or flutters of hysteria may form into bedlam, in the same way as a few football hooligans can fan a crowd into a riotous mass.

Those with a disturbed psyche do sense and prod the same within us. The insane can disturb the psychic barriers we have carefully built in order to separate us from our primitive forces. In marginalising the insane, we deny what is inherent in all of us. Not only may people with lifelong mental issues, and those with more acute disorders, bring great joy to those who welcome them, they serve to challenge our hypocrisy; they remind us of our commonalities by manifesting primal energies in an exaggerated way.

The more the underlying source of psychological disturbance is appreciated, the quicker the subversive stigma of psychosis, which comes from ignorance and fear, will dissipate and its creative value be realised. Rather than cast/outcast a few scapegoats to carry these primal forces for us, we might appreciate such people for what they can teach us.

*

We are not so different. Reactive, impulsive emotions and urges surface when our survival feels threatened. When daily supplies run short, whether it is petrol or bread, we want to get to the head of the queue. Just think what could happen if we had to compete with others in order to assuage our thirst - all hell might be let loose. Scratch the surface and we find that the savage lurks within everyone.

If our physical life is at stake such instinctual effects are vital protection. But generally, an emotional outburst is a reflex action to what seems to be an attack on our fragile sense of self. We regress to our initial experience of, and thrust for, true self expression and autonomy. Repressed emotions have not been honed into conscious feeling states. Thus, in their discharge, there is no mediation by complementary balancing agents. They are out of our control. Even when we manage to keep these forces down, they remain active within the shadow and leak out. Let us look at some examples of such reactions, in view of the line, albeit wiggly, between neurosis and psychosis.

For instance, in defending a perceived public cause such as war or mass outrage at a societal injustice, a profusion of repressed emotions come to the surface which often stem from emotional injuries in childhood. Hitler's barbarous incitement to genocide, according to Miller (1987), sprang from his primal wound and others were carried along by the same collective energy. Land and communities are ravaged when seething fury, fuelled by unconscious primal hurts, flies under the banner of heroes struggling for the common good. Gratuitous violence is a means for, and a symptom of, dehumanisation. We discharge that which we have disowned and to which we have been subjected.

A vicious punch in a game of rugby, from a man who is seen as a law-abiding citizen both on and off the field, is a release of primal energy. A reaction thought as totally out of character is often a short blast of psychotic behaviour. His normal neurotic defence could be to retroflect his anger and get himself injured, or to incite his team mates to be overly aggressive when tackling the opposition.

At the neurotic level, the line between consciously channelling primitive forces and acting them out unwittingly is obscure; whereas when we exhibit extreme behaviour which surprises us, it is generally an unconscious impulse which has broken through from our psychotic layer. The deeper the split, the more obvious is such release, to an observer, as the contrast is greater.

A woman who generally appears to one and all to take diligent care of her spouse, could find herself ripping up her errant husband's clothes. She only momentarily dropped her neurotic cover, 'lost it', had a lapse in her usual demeanour and reacted overtly to extreme provocation. Typically she protects herself from sensing and expressing feelings of betrayal and intense hatred of him by 'accidentally' scorching his shirt when ironing or by being 'too tired' to make love. Such reasonable excuses show a neurotic use of a substitute object to repress reality. Her mad rage of wanting to rip him apart or kill off his libido is well disguised, therefore difficult to confront, by these more neurotic passive aggressive traits.

Slow drips of carping criticism and systematic deprivation are common neurotic practices which will surely and slowly break down a person whose core self assurance is not developed. These are diluted forms of torture and brainwashing, both of which could be considered psychopathic acts. Either we know the torturer which lives in our dungeon or we meet it out there in life.

Take our neurotic concern with body image. We might think nothing of wearing uncomfortable clothes, of undergoing grueling diets and even submitting to painful plastic surgery. But we might be shocked if, out of the blue, we debase ourselves by accepting or dishing out perverse sadistic treatment directly.

Sadomasochism exemplifies how love is polluted by domination, humiliation and pain, particularly when it comes to sex. Where there is some element of control and agreement between partners in this practice, it could be considered a neurotic predilection, even a safe outlet which is just titillating fun. But it might become obsessive and dangerously out of hand.

Whatever the level, destructive behaviour represents a primary attack on self. If we were treated as a thing to be exploited in childhood, this way of engaging with another, or indeed with ourselves, may seem acceptable.

*

Let us now consider whether we have a preponderance towards narcissism and then compare it to more borderline characteristics - bearing in mind that the models portrayed emphasise more extreme, therefore more obvious, modes of behaviour. By recognising such tendencies in ourselves, however, we might blend the bands between what is irrational and what is sane.

If we lean strongly towards narcissism, we will have an inflated adapted self so shored up with rigid walls that we are quite cut off from our elementary nature. Indeed often, the more successful our public persona, the wider the gulf. But we would rather feel that we are someone special, however false, than nobody. Therefore, maintaining a seemingly perfect lifestyle is our most important ongoing goal. However, as we have given up living our truth, such measures provide only a temporary feeling of well being and security. Stirring below is the feeling that we are a fraud and that people might see through us.

This formation is called secondary narcissism as it arises out of our primary narcissism never being satisfied when young. The hard won shield which covers our narcissistic wound will be held on to tenaciously as, underneath, we are raw. Consequently, we pick up the smallest nuance which to us seems to threaten our image and mode of survival – the neurotic fear of persecution.

Naturally, such slights might have some substance. But they can be so highly exaggerated and distorted by us that our reaction crescendos into paranoia – the psychotic terror of annihilation. The core self is barely clinging onto life. The slightest hint of it being exposed disturbs the bastions of our subconscious; for this might ignite the deepest emotions, still simmering way down below, which were evoked at the time of our earliest wounding.

Interweave these forces with subsequent similarly threatening experiences and the result is confusion. It may feel as if an early scenario is happening in the present moment. We see our partner or boss cold-eyed or raging before us but we will feel as if our primary carer is admonishing us. For the psychotic there is no 'as if'. We believe that our enemy is brandishing a knife or that our bête noire is sprouting a tail and horns and is really out there after our blood.

Be aware that not all narcissists appear superior. Some of us might overdose on 'humbleness'. Being in an inferior place seems to win us some attention, therefore we wear our primary neediness on our sleeve. We play the innocent victim, particularly when, in our voracious urge to feed off others, people back away or turn against us. We dare not acknowledge our own predatory power.

With both sides of narcissism, grandiose or small, one way of maintaining some sense of selfhood is to depersonalise others. As was done to us in infancy, we turn others into objects and, often unawarely, we systematically try and destroy those who do not satisfy our wants, which are never ending. Our true self is emotionally starving and spiritually impoverished since we cannot really believe, take in and hold on to another's approval.

Usually, the social mask shows the exact opposite of the shadow. The person who wears a mantle of grandiosity often chooses a partner who can take on his or her 'inferior' or depressed side so that this seems to remain outside. As a couple, they give the impression of being very different but at their roots lies the common primal wound of a broken relationship with the core self. Two lost babes in the wood living on opposite sides of a tree facing outwards so that no real engagement can take place. It is what they are used to.

Those with the mask of Narcissus see in the mirror

only their adapted selves. This outward reflection encases their inner hollowness - the void where their unacceptable, therefore undeveloped, true self should flourish. They have built a survival structure, with all its neurotic defences, which does its best to avoid the loneliness of being separated from their innermost being.

A client of mine literally modelled herself on a celebrity. She styled her hair accordingly, matched her lips and face paint, copied her clothes and mimicked her mannerisms. My client was in her sixties and was becoming increasingly distraught because her self esteem was governed by her appearance, which was seriously declining in her eyes. When pain surfaced in a session, she quickly wiped away the tears for fear that her mascara would run. Rather than dig deep into her psychic splits so that they might heal, she literally and figuratively got out her mirror in order to apply more make-up over the ever widening cracks which were appearing at face level.

Image was all and she sought constant affirmation to sustain this. She tried so hard to please people and she saw her apparent self-lessness as a virtue. Yet with little inner substance of her own, she sapped other's vitality. Admiration is a poor substitute for love and understanding. Everyone missed out on embracing the real her – a sad case of an abandoned soul.

With the limited and self-referant view of Narcissus comes a rigidity in perceptions. These are often split into 'vices and virtues' as the challenge of ambivalence is hard to bear. At a deep level, we know only too well what it is like to feel wrong and that we will fall apart if we let go, therefore we can be obsessionally controlling and controlled.

With people diagnosed as having a *narcissistic personality disorder*, considered psychotic, there are persistent disturbances of the whole being. They are right, even if they are self-flagellating, and woe betide anyone who tries to prove them wrong. Difference is felt like an attack.

The way our psyche pivots around maintaining some sense of identity, even hanging onto a false construction rather than none at all, goes to show just how fragile our hold on sanity is. Without a secure attachment to our true self, at the back of our mind there is a door to the unknown which can so easily become unhinged if opened wide - and we, at some level, know it.

*

If borderline characteristics predominate, we have much weaker boundaries and a more fluid sense of self. Unlike the narcissist's fixed construction, the borderline configuration is extremely open and is less able to use compensatory devices of coping under stress. It is as if we are flailing about in mid-air without anything to hold onto. We and the world are fragmented. Everything is contradictory and primary impulses are near to the surface.

Therefore, we are given to overwhelming fantasies. Life is hell. We are acutely aware of our sensitivity, inner emptiness, feelings of abandonment and of being misunderstood. Having been given mixed messages, passed around to different carers or possessed completely by another as a youngster, when we close our eyes the outer world disappears.

One man I remember well. He had developed a split between the normal neurotic and a psychotic personality, both of which somehow managed to operate, albeit antagonistically, at the same time. He was so keen for me to make a connection with his meandering mind.

I have found that it is as important to concede when true contact is impossible as it is to honour times when there is concordance with a person such as he. With little outer persona to protect, while fearing honesty, he also relishes it. If someone with a borderline typology is ever to achieve a modicum of trust towards another, he, in particular, needs to know the truth of his perception.

People classified with a *borderline personality disorder* feel they are everywhere and nowhere. There is little pretence. They might be covered in confusion but their hostility, or affection, is obvious. What you see is what you get. Despite being challenging to be with, as they are intense, unstable and unpredictable, there may be moments when a genuine connection is made. What strikes me is that, although less adapted to what is considered normal life, in their openness they are nearer to their unformed true self, even if they do not have the wherewithal to hold this self together.

    The degree and extent of the different symptoms we display, together with how we perceive ourselves and the world, determine how we are seen, approached and typecast by others. Borderline traits are more commonly deemed psychotic therefore those who manifest them are more marginalised; whereas narcissistic behaviour, even when encapsulated within a narcissistic personality disorder, is generally considered to be more acceptable. This is largely due to society depending on people keeping up the appearance of order. A fixed point, however distorted, gives some sense of orientation and security; whereas the borderline's fluidity reveals what is ordinarily hidden and can blow the cover off conformity. It makes you think.

* * *

Section C Coming to our true senses

The psyche has intrinsic currents of purpose which are essentially ingenious. Its workings are a constant marvel to me, although often evident only in retrospect. Here, we will explore societal attitudes to madness and then, how we may help our self and humanity by attending to our primal forces.

Much madness Is divinest Sense –
To a discerning eye –
Much Sense - the starkest madness –
'Tis the Majority
In this, as All, prevail –
Assent - and you are sane –
Demur - You're straightway dangerous –
And handled with a Chain   Dickenson, 1992

    Society in general is afraid of its constitution disintegrating. Being fragile, agreement between what is a normal and abnormal mental state is vehemently defended.

But this censorship is so inhibiting to progress because, when conscious, extraordinary emotions and impulses can be regulated and used as a resource for self realisation. Therefore, the psychotic laboratory, where familiar frames of reference and senses are extended and amplified, is certainly worthy of closer inspection.

The magical world of the 'simple minded' child is not compromised by expectations. Thus like Alice, who went into Wonderland and *Through the Looking Glass* (Carroll, 1993) to meet psychotic elements, if we enter this world of nonsensical dialogue and riddles with an open heart and curious mind, we can spot glimpses of truth. Logic can come out of the most absurd behaviour. Rich insights are to be found in the splintered mirror of illusion and delusion.

Once, I considered the insane to be well cushioned from the trials of the normal world. I had imagined their life to be like a fantasy play in which they could reinvent themselves into parts which eased their pain considerably. This was certainly a protective illusion on my part as I was to find out, the hard way, that they were more likely to be stuck in a hellish place.

Making the insane into figures of fun is another defensive device. There is a sense of safety when the majority unites against the minority. It is not so long ago that the physically and mentally impaired were exhibited in freak shows, as a source of amusement and fascination. They still add a frisson to the classic tale in which sounds of wailing are said to come from the attic.

Tragedy and comedy work well together in literature as in life. Humour can lighten the unbearable and mask the fear. Yet a manic edge to laughter can be detected circling around the subject of madness. It certainly relieves the one who instigates the humour. But the object of such mirth can feel mocked and further alienated from mankind - the classic scapegoat.

However, when coupled with compassion and understanding, humour may break the hold of psychotic elements by defusing their intensity. The paradox is that by creating distance and so greater objectivity, they are more easily integrated into the self. I am not advocating that laughing in the face of madness is the cure - far from it - rather that humour sometimes helps heal the rifts from and within psychosis.

Finding a way across this divide, however, is like walking through a minefield. It took many attempts before my therapist used the tool of humour to good effect and I was, at last, able to catch a funny side to my ravings. Momentarily, we made a connection, albeit very shaky, in what felt like mutual disarmament and truth.

Just as the comic is the master of disguise and freer of depression, so the creative genius or visionary mystic is closely allied to the madman. They are on the same continuum. Where would we be without the artistic temperament of poets like Byron, composers such as Schumman and far-seeing painters like Van Gogh? (Redfield Jamison, 1993) Similarly, Winston Churchill channelled his manic and depressive tendencies into an indomitable will and depth of emotion which inspired and saved a nation from being conquered. Awesome creativity has come out of those suffering from severe mood swings, affording gifts to the world which have expanded our horizons.

The intensest light of reason and revelation combined, can not shed such blazonings upon the deeper truths in man as sometimes proceed from his own profoundest gloom. Utter darkness is then his light, and cat-like he distinctly sees all objects through a medium which is mere blindness to common vision. (Melville, 1992)

The genius and the visionary are bathed in light and lauded with praise, while the madman is seen as a figure of darkness, is shunned and abused. They are perceived by most to be at either end of the spectrum. But rather than polarise them in this way, each might be recognised for tapping far reaching elements. Yet, while both struggle with life and death principles of self and the cosmos, the mad are unable to boil their rush of experiences down into an easily communicable and comprehensive form. There is no consciousness of self, no organising principle with which to weave them into a coherent whole - they remain scrambled activity; whereas with a strong enough attachment to the core self, these disparate elements can be arranged into a synthesis which brings new meaning - the genius, or visionary, masters them.

Plato considers *'ritualized madness, where chaotic and*

seemingly insane experiences and behaviour lead to deeper levels of order.' Assumptions obscure original connection. Psychic flashes stimulate what may seem irrational perceptions which then fall into more fulsome organisation.

Genius is a light which makes the darkness visible, like lightning's flash, which perchance shatters the temple of knowledge itself. (Thoreau, 1992)

The root of the word 'genius' essentially means that which is an original factor or spirit which resides in us, hence 'gene, genie and genuine'. It is through going to our genuine roots that we release our inherent spirit.

Many beliefs and behaviours which, in the past, were perfectly acceptable are now considered crazy and people once thought as insane have since been hailed as legendary figures. Similarly, the conforming masses feel threatened by the genius and the visionary, but as time goes by, their ideas are revered and the eccentric's individuality is tolerated, even envied by some.

Thus, although we continue to fete the intellectual and scientific, now when someone speaks from their heart it is more often well received than it used to be. Staying on a more optimistic note, with this greater freedom to voice our true feelings, the stigma and fear attached to those seeking therapy for neurotic symptoms is lessening, therefore the obdurate divide between the neurotic and psychotic 'us' and 'them' might soften also.

*

Psychosis can be viewed through many lenses. It can be construed as simply inborn, coming from early trauma, a physiological phenomenon, a weakness, a totally negative psychic disorder and/or part of the human condition. One observation proffered (Nelson, 1994) is that psychosis might be a spiritual emergency, a spiritual emergence which has failed due to insufficient holding.

While I welcome this view, as it honours what may be the initial thrust in madness, I am looking through the reverse side of this particular lens. I see that, when base elements have not been contained and transformed in childhood, psychosis is a prerequisite for true spiritual emergence.

Current technology means that the world is shrinking and while cosmic and ordinary reality are drawing closer together, with the increase in global migration, other mores and beliefs are influencing local communities. Many cultures balance spiritual development alongside material growth. For example, in the Hindu tradition, focus on self actualisation through education, work and family commitments is encouraged in the first half of life. Later, respect and honour are shown to those who then relinquish these duties and go travelling to further expand their self via both primitive and spiritual avenues.

Throughout life, vistas change. Severe setbacks, like disablement, loss of home or established role, and major calamities, like flood or war, can mean that the world we once knew and relied on has disappeared for ever. Traumas remind us of our impermanence. Similarly, fortuitous events, such as parenthood and new found fame and fortune, can also challenge familiar ways of seeing things. A radical event often uncovers a mass of unconscious matter. For instance, in losing a long-term partner, we might find that we are left with those projections which they once carried for us.

There is some inevitable, slow breakdown of mind and body in the aging process which can bring up a resurgence of our dependency and fragility. Often material objects and worldly diversions no longer satisfy and there may be only memories to live off. Of course, faith in some existence in the hereafter can soften the thought of our future demise. But as the shadow of mortality lingers close at hand, there can be a mellowing of rigid structures so that we feel the charge from soul demanding the truth of our self is manifest on earth. Rather than fade as our mental and physical functions diminish, its fire shines more brightly.

Ideally, this growth towards wholeness should have begun at birth, even perhaps at conception. Failing that, the earlier the breakdown of subsequently assumed adaptations, the easier. The deeper and older the wound, generally the harder and longer the process of uncovering and healing it, since convoluted layers of suffering and corresponding defences will have accumulated over the passing years. But it is never too late to reassess our priorities and realise that the search for self worth may vie with, or precede, the urge to accumulate material assets. As inhabitants of this troubled globe, we are all faced with putting a price on our personal and collective well being.

*

Each one of us makes a difference on planet earth as it is a living breathing entity of which we are part. Just as energy from collective issues influences us as individuals, we also radiate many unconscious effects which cannot be quantified. We are terrified of 'evil', the terrorists and weapons of mass destruction seen in the collective 'out there'. Rarely do we face the equivalent forces in our personal shadow. Yet we come from the same resources and fundamental urges are at the root of our continuing disharmony.

As with global warming and stockpiling waste, we can feed the mass of hostility and persecution which might obliterate the soul of the world. Or, we could respect and attend to the needs of our intrapsychic devouring and warring elements and thereby limit widespread conflict.

People who have taken the pains to really listen to terrorists report that it is the humiliation of being disregarded which fosters violent retaliation, with such tragic consequences. Hell raising anarchists can either be combated with equal force, met head on, or they might arouse a heartfelt awareness as to the intensity of mankind's innate need to be seen and heard. Reaching out at this core level may be the supreme way to come into peaceful coexistence.

Firm structures of government are being torn down. Such upheaval, and potential reform, is reflected in the transitional space between the child and adult world, when teenagers are prone to try to put the world to rights, to challenge the fabric of their foundations and to broaden their mind through travel. This *liminal* state, when all that has been held true and safe is shaken, is similar to the turmoil felt when wavering on the threshold of madness.

Schizophrenia most often strikes in the late teens and

early twenties and the attraction towards the drug, alternative health and mystical cultures is also a sign of the craving to explore the further reaches of the psyche when young.

What is unconscious constantly seeks outlets in order to survive and can endanger self and society when not contained. Indeed, current statistics show that, by the age of fifteen, one in three youngsters has taken cannabis and that early drug use dramatically increases the risk of mental illness. As so many juveniles seem to be using mind-expanding drugs to go there anyway, why not channel their psyche's pull to good effect? One way is to experiment with consciousness using artificial means to produce ecstatic or diabolic fantasies of the world. The alternative is to work with elemental psychic matter in order to come to grips with internal conflict systems.

The state provides centres of detention for addicts to detoxify, as well as for criminals and the mentally insane. The inmates are often mixed together due to the confusion between desire for rebellion and extreme alternative cultures, with an existential need. In these institutions what is evident to the discerning eye, alongside the tendency to attract punishment and inflict self destruction as a re-creation of primary wounding, is the burning issue of self emergence.

Perhaps if the rest of society understood better why the younger generation is set on playing with 'magic potions' like Alice in Wonderland and why they adopt this devil-may-care attitude, without envying it, they might support enterprises which could transform this thrust. While intervention in cases of addiction and abuse is commendable, prevention of the cycle continuing into future generations is certainly a noble cause.

There are excellent counselling schemes for disturbed youngsters and 'youth at risk' ventures. However, these resources are comparatively few and far between. Society needs such initiatives to be more widely and freely available so that all juveniles may 're-vision' what is really valuable to them. Both the well-behaved and dissident alike could benefit from a liberal yet boundaried place in which to explore a rich diversity of ideas; an arena to share and embrace those principles which resonate; a space to gain emotional access to their deepest being.

But while having a rite of passage into adulthood might well appeal to teenagers, there are so many more seemingly exciting things to do before settling down. Perhaps we remember when, with our whole life ahead of us, we imagined that most personal problems could be rectified by changing our environment, partner, job or lifestyle. Invariably, we acted as if external circumstances, rather than internal psychic dynamics, determined whether we were successful and happy.

Many adolescents, and immature adults for that matter, see a baby as the remedy for filling the empty vessel which, behind the front, they feel themselves to be. It seems easier to make a child the centre of their life than to find their own core centre. Seeing themselves mirrored in the infant they produced, they suppose that the seed of their loins will provide them with a sense of existence and future. Their offspring is deemed an extension which completes them and helps anchor them in the world.

But who is mirroring and holding the baby's selfhood? Not the primary carer with an inner child's needs. It may be only when extreme pain and difficulty continue to blight our life that we are forced to examine how the relationship we have with ourselves affects our outer world

The most practical and lasting solution, to present unrest and further destabilisation in society, is to bring 'emotional literacy' into our schools; not just on the curriculum but to underpin the whole of school life. Without this vital groundwork, to quote a wise and soulful assistant head teacher who has educated children for forty years, 'Our world is doomed'.

*

Thus we return to the challenge of tackling mental health at source, when many who care for the young have embraced neither the rudiments of self development, nor their own primary attachment issues. Such work has to begin somehow, somewhere and soon since current statistics show that one in five youngsters will develop some form of mental disorder.

Please note that the commitment to and extensiveness of such inner work is commensurate with the severity of our primal wound. Thus those with a strong inner core will bring about a positive change just by continuing to mature. Also, this commission should not be taken as a licence to act out psychotic elements but rather to prompt some serious consideration as to whether to invest in such a life choice. Furthermore, the initiative is not just confined to parents, teachers and therapists as we are all guardians of children to some extent.

For the world as a whole to integrate their primal forces is an utopian dream. Yet the blight of primal wounding, which has reproduced through the ages, might thus be interrupted. What a magnificent prospect for humanity to contemplate. Maybe one truly enlightened day, those who brave and accommodate the psychotic dimension will receive encouragement and due regard for their personal work and concurrent service to healing the splits in mankind.

Diabolical times call for drastic measures and it is the outlandish brainstorm which generates a fertile mind and so might fan debate on adopting a more radical approach to our mental well being. Of course, the world would not survive if everyone was going through a psychotic crisis, although presently the planet does seem to be showing signs of a collective breakdown.

A psychological take on current global destabilisation is that basic laws are clashing with neurotic defences of order and control against terror of annihilation. Science conjectures that when two parallel worlds collide, there is a big bang which gives birth to new life. So it is when our psyche's conscious and dense unconscious spheres crash.

Like the stars which form from the exploding core of a super nova, *'We must have chaos within to give birth to a dancing star'* (Nietzsche,1969). The inference follows that from a bout of mental dissolution our vital self can coalesce and emerge in all its brilliance and vibrancy. Accordingly, in order for the spark from soul to ignite a powerful enough life force for ongoing synthesis of self, our psyche might need to be thoroughly shaken not stirred.

Anarchic forces may have to loosen up still further before we awaken fully to the dire need for us, as individuals, to take responsibility for the future state of our world. If we are to bring our currently unstable planet into harmony, it is crucial that we recognise the seriousness of what is at stake, as we might only seize the moment, and the part we play in it, in the nick of time. Perhaps it will take further world catastrophes for us to come to our true senses so that the fruits of such realisation will be harvested for future generations. Many dancing stars may be born out of universal chaos - as above, so below.

✳

Thus let us consider the structure of our psyche, and its possible deconstruction, and whether there is conflict within.

Generally, our outer persona changes according to our environment. Therefore a workmate may see in us a different aspect, or *subpersonality*, from that which our partner sees. Each subpersonality fulfils a role which demonstrates particular wants, qualities and emotions. For example, the sportsman might exhibit physical strength, tenacity and desire to succeed by competition. Alternatively, feelings of love, sacrifice and belonging may be engendered when in a father role.

Ideally, all our subpersonalities will be working in harmony to manifest our true essence. Thus we will be able to disengage from all the various parts we play and enjoy just being. To be truly alive really means being able to connect with a still and vibrant sense of self. When we can switch attention to the self who is experiencing what is happening within us, this presence brings inner strength as, whatever happens to us in life, we have this constant factor.

For instance, a man could lose his worldly roles of businessman, husband, father and sportsman, without it threatening his sense of rightful existence. He is not dependent on outward manifestations of his inner qualities. His self worth and dignity survive such divestment.

As well as this configuration of our psyche, we will have collated and condensed experiences from those times which have induced a particular feeling state. The inferiority complex is well known. Less obvious is its neurotic defence, the superiority complex. Some feelings of low self esteem may remain conscious to the grandiose self image, while others stay in the pre-conscious.

Generally, the kernel of truth to both these complexes springs from the primal wound. But its core may be so heavily impacted with moments when we have felt belittled and ashamed of ourself, that it requires an equally strong impact for all the distorted and vital properties to burst forth, so that these are felt directly and eventually clarified.

Of course, we can work stage by stage back to the original wounding. But what has congealed into a mass cannot be extricated slowly without contaminating material seeping into healthy formations. Similarly, new authentic elements will attach themselves to what remains of the adapted self structure. We are apparently better but resistance to the psychotic layer is strengthened.

The alternative is to lose this controlling function, to leave it behind with our more worldly associations, and to descend into personal chaos. Rather than slowly de-integrate psychic constructions, these disintegrate. Madness represents a confused version of primitive forces and primary violation compounded with complexes which have arisen from these sources. Often vented from recesses deep in the viscera, all may feel so alien that they can only come as delusional thoughts, voices and hallucinations. Thereby our core power is released so that long lasting recovery and deep personal growth may take place.

Both ways of reaching the core have their dangers and are essentially painful. Even a gentle probe of the primal wound will hurt. While healing is associated with comfort, with alleviation and sublimating painful experiences, some of us may have to feel the very worst - the utter desolation and emptiness of non being - to feel truly the best. Such a demanding and gruelling process can be the ultimate choice between living a lie and truly living.

*

When madness touches us, we can be taken back to the original 'death' of our true being and, potentially, to the birth of who we are meant to be. If the primal elements scared or shamed our carers so were repressed, they may continue to hold the same charge for us. The pressure to discharge them can build up to such a degree that it is like a time bomb waiting to go off.

The fallout from the subsequent explosion is enough to send our family and friends scattering. They might exclaim, 'Where has the person we once knew and loved gone? She is not herself; she is a shadow of what she used to be.' How right they are. Were they to see us in the formative stage of becoming a much richer human being, their support would be invaluable. There is nothing like a good friend to help ground us in life.

But more likely, people around us will be disturbed by our struggle and will seem to threaten our difficult metamorphosis. Therefore, in order to examine and lick our wound clean, we may have no alternative than to become something of a recluse - which furthers the sense of abandonment, aloneness and desolation as in our primal split from self.

Solitary confinement, according to prisoners, is the most decimating of punishments, outstripping all other forms of physical and psychological tortures. Perverse as it may be, like the sadist-masochist dyad, interrogation and violence brings some engagement; whereas, when condemned to be set apart from all human contact over a long period, it is as if we are forgotten, our existence denied and we have disappeared. Without another living soul to relate to, we can but come close to a non being state.

Yet it might be solely out of this terrible state of alienation that our true self can free itself. In the wild and barren environment, there is room to shift, stretch and tend to our life force. Self-centredness takes on a new meaning since here, we may find the centre of our self. Recognising and stepping into the real power of our individuating being can be a daunting prospect. But when we go into the void to redeem our original self from our primal roots, we may realise that this is what we have been looking for all our life. In our internal wilderness, we might find the true rootstock of our spiritual inheritance.

'We grow strong in the broken places', and in breaking down into our primitive elements innately strong healing forces may be released. Rather than see madness solely as a destructive force which rises unbidden, we can choose to harness its positive and creative nature.

Our soul will struggle against seemingly insurmountable odds to win its rightful place in the world, as in Dante's (1998) journey into forbidding territory. A few are prepared to struggle through extraordinary adversity when only a sliver of hope of redeeming their inherent self remains.

For better or worse, I count myself as one of these. So much of this time, I stayed at the limit of endurance, wishing for it all to be over rather than striving forward - direction has little meaning in psychosis as there are no real horizons, no ends. It takes us to areas where we encounter some terrible but natural phenomena which lie at the edge of human experience. We enter dimensions, lost, forgotten or seemingly inaccessible to most of mankind.

There are many reasons given as to why man braves uncharted territory - for the glory, the euphoric rush in danger, because 'it is there' and in order to discover valuable resources. I have staked my claim. My flag is flying on this far reaching terrain, having found my self through the realms of madness.

Yet it is more for the cause of psychosis, and its potential outcome, that I seek recognition, rather than for a heroic self. Indeed, I question the part my will power did play in this venture, as its blind force was directed more against me than toward my effort to survive. It was more like the fear of my psychotic forces which drove me and the subliminal pull of soul which kept me going.

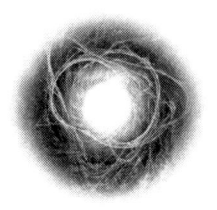

Chapter 7

An Empowering or Disempowering Therapeutic Holding

Section A Seeing what is needed

We all yearn to be clearly seen and heard, to be accepted for who we really are and to belong.
  Please, Hear What I'm Not Saying
Don't be fooled by the face I wear, for I wear a thousand masks,
And none of them is me...
Beneath dwells the real me in confusion, in fear, in aloneness,...
I'm afraid that deep-down I'm nothing, and that I'm just no good
And that you will see this, and reject me...
But you've got to really help me. You've got to hold out your hand.
Only you can call me into aliveness...
Each time you try to understand because you really care,
My heart begins to grow wings, very feeble wings, but wings...
Please try to beat down these walls with firm hands
But gentle hands – for a child is very sensitive...
Who am I you may wonder?
I am someone you know very well,
For I am every man you meet, and I am every woman you meet,
And I am you, also.

Finn, 1966

While much in this chapter applies to usual practice in psychotherapy and analysis, the first two sections focus on therapeutic approaches which are of particular importance to anyone journeying into the furthest reaches of the psyche. They also suggest those to be wary of - mostly learnt from my mistakes. Then more of the dynamics between my therapist and myself follow and the chapter ends with me hitting rock bottom and finding my turning point. Few might need to go there and fewer may choose to - but some might find themselves struggling with psychosis regardless while others may begin to know what the primitive psyche can be like through association.

Most people in therapy discover many new aspects of themselves by working through their neuroses, with maybe only an occasional and brief psychotic moment. Not everyone who looks at their unconscious will hit a psychotic patch. It is certainly the exception and not what normally happens. This is why I draw mainly on my personal experience to illustrate how it is possible to cohere psychotic material and form a substantial self.

*

I believe that mine is a cautionary tale and reveals what is fundamentally dangerous when exploring the profundity of emotional, mental, physical and spiritual structures. Thus, I will now sketch out the first nine months of my psychotic incursion using the analogy of the force of water, so as to indicate such movement.

Having taken some steps down into the dark well of my unconscious, I dived in. The deeper I went, the more I felt dragged by an insistent current until I could no longer fight its force but only let it take me where it would. This flow continually changed direction, speed and form and so I felt as though I was being forced along narrow straits of manmade canals, torn over river beds, tossed high in fountains and thrown back down waterfalls. Eventually, pummelled and pulverised, it was as if I spilled into cesspools and was absorbed by bogs until the water washed through me; I dissolved with trickling streams into splashing rivers, ever nearing the font head. I was being pulled back to a watery source, to the oceans from where rain clouds form and let loose their thundery canons and copious tears. I was returning to formlessness.

However, despite being carried by this momentum further than I had intended, the initial thrust was mine. Having gone head first, I had some sense of direction. Therefore, every so often, I was able to come up for air ... only to sink down again, until I realised that my reserves were spent. Now was the time to free myself from the powerful currents and to swim back to the surface. So far so good. This was the watershed where I needed to return to terra firma in order to reform my experiences and to redefine my self.

This first stage in my plunge to the depths was made within a strong therapeutic container, a vessel well-used to psychosis. But then I was lured, in the hope of rescue, by other seemingly expert swimmers in the psychic seas. These therapists, however, turned out to be more like lifeguards intent on showing off their muscles rather than on bringing me back to life.

I was gasping, shaking but I saw arms reaching out which might lift me clear. Instead, they pushed me over the edge, thrust me back, so I plummeted into the fathomless deep without any means to break my fall. Unprepared for this enforced immersion, I was sucked down into the vortex of a whirlpool where sensations do not link but fuse together. Stunned, I had no chance.

*

I cannot emphasise enough to those who are on a deep psychic exploration, particularly to those whose trust was misplaced when young, that it is imperative that we stay with only 'deeply-wounded healers' who have discovered their core self through the psychotic realms. Had I realised this fact earlier, my psychic immersion and subsequent recovery would have been less protracted and more manageable – of this I am certain.

Nevertheless, such was my pathology, whatever therapeutic vessel I had used for my descent, I would of necessity have dropped into turbulent waters. Of course, someone who experiences an emotional relatedness and has a supportive milieu, who is self sufficient thus able to step back, disidentify and reflect, will find it easier to survive a psychic depth charge. But I was a bit short on these inclusion factors at the time.

For those of us similarly bereft, such a descent might be safe enough with a therapist who is familiar with psychosis within himself. We may sense that he has done it, therefore so can we. Then if some extreme psychic forces do hit us, we are more likely to establish a life-line between the two of us which leads to the light of our being. Like a sustaining mother, he will hold our fragile self for us while we are submerged in elemental material.

Thus a subtle link is maintained with our psychotic world of delusion, which also holds the secret ingredients for our healing, until such time as we can take on board and engage with a more meaningful reality. For a lasting and profound reform of self, both parties may sometimes have to submit to the turbulent deep.

Those clients with a deep primal wound might be restricted and, like myself, be further damaged by this lack of innermost appreciation of the psychotic function in the therapeutic world. Although I refer to my own case as it unfolds throughout the pages, I would not bring this issue to the fore if I had not witnessed how others had been affected by it. I am not alone in this experience but few come through with a vital enough sense of self. For those who do, not many have the wherewithal to explain the cause and effect of their inadequate treatment and if they have, few are willing to risk their reputation.

When fragmented, I came into contact with so many practitioners whose power was not 'in-formed' by the integration of their psychotic forces. They were not used to accommodating these energies, thus their projected psychoses compounded in me. With me, they had no secure, regulating boundaries or procedures in place because they had never embraced the dark underworld for themselves. They were out of their depth. But for ages I was utterly foxed by these therapeutic set-ups since they were so like those of my primary family. I could not break the inculcated taboo against independent thought and thereby see the corresponding flaws.

But then came an incident which, although baffling at the time, soon became a real eye opener. Despite being plagued by psychotic episodes, I was continuing with my professional development and I attempted to describe what was happening to me to a high ranking member of staff. Referring to the training team, she shrugged, waved her hand in a dismissive way and pronounced in a sententious tone, 'We've all been there'. My heart dropped to the pit of my stomach, from where I knew this was not so. Had her statement been true, I am sure that I would have sensed in the depth of my being such mutuality. Also, these teachers would have been handling me very differently.

However, I gave no pithy retort to the trainer's comment and neither did her colleague who expressed incredulity only in her gawping face - the power of speech was denied us both. Any vestige of courage deserted me. As it was, my rage and terror, which are part and parcel of psychosis, had been fuelled by their inappropriate treatment for some time. But I still needed to believe that what they were doing to me was for my own good and came from a caring place. The bare and painful facts were too awful to face.

I was easy pickings and they, in my visions, were vultures who were stripping away my torn flesh to render insensible my vital organs. How I see it now is that my crisis was evoking in these professionals a fear of their cover being blown and their psychotic parts being agitated. If I was exterminated, they were safe. I had to go. Ranks were closed, as the truth of my primal nightmare challenged and discomposed their false self constructs.

Of course, for my part, I was dramatising my childhood environment and projecting out my fear and rage. But most of what I experienced at the hands of these trainers I needed like a hole in the head - a common cliché but only too real for me since hallucinating a hatchet splitting open my skull.

Just a couple of trainers saw the potential benefit of my experience in psychosis and that it might help balance the panoply of transpersonal principals that paraded in this organisation. These sagacious individuals who had broken the mould were strong enough to embrace the tenet that there was strength in diversity. But they did not last long in this narcissistic environment.

The treacherous waters closed over my head. I was meant to carry the reflection of the organisation's collective shadow away with me, to disappear, without a mark left behind to show where I had been. But I was to return - although it took me over a year to summon up enough strength to do so.

∗

Let us go to the mainstream for a while since, on the whole, people look for a quick tonic. Indeed, the majority find their way through life without professional help and they deem it satisfying enough. Of those people who admit to having difficulty coping, few want the upheaval of long and intensive therapy.

Instead, many find short term counselling very helpful. When in a crisis, it gives them a clearer view from which they can make some decisions. For example, bereavement counselling eases the way through the important stages of grieving. It patches people up sufficiently to get on with their lives. For some couples, 'marriage guidance' has improved their relationship and/or provided the impetus to make a necessary break. Cognitive behavioural therapy is popular as it can readily identify those old life scripts which continue to limit and to cause distress. It produces fast about turns for many who are stuck in a difficult situation and frees them to return to normal life. But however mindful, some remain troubled as such proactive procedures tend to plaster over the top of earlier, deeper wounds.

Other people turn to self-help groups, such as Alcoholics Anonymous and Survivors of Childhood Sexual Abuse, which give much needed support and resolution to many a blighted life. These groups are not enough for everyone, though. What happens is that some participants become so identified as a survivor, a reactive formation against their victim polarity, that their history lives on, fed by their zeal. The damage is borne like a cross and/or a curse.

Like a bee to nectar, all those who feel uncherished

may be drawn to a friendly soul who listens, shows empathy and respect. Indeed, once a week I had some valuable support, outside my regular therapy sessions, from someone who acted like a comfy cushion on which I could lay my troubles. I then would reciprocate. This mutual arrangement is called 'co-counselling'.

A few of my friends have found Prozac a godsend (Kramer, 1996) and they could not understand why I took the harder long-term route. They said that Prozac gave them a lift, a brighter outlook on life and, moreover, that their depression had been just a passing phase. But the effect did not last. They continued to have mini-breakdowns and needed these pick-me-ups, or they became physically ill. One friend considered therapy, one went into it briefly and another made a commitment to sorting her life out with a therapist.

*

Looking at deeper therapy, we find that most models include techniques for unravelling the psyche. For example, chair work can be a dramatic way of tapping the unconscious. This is the *Gestalt* (Perls, 1972) method where the client changes seats as she takes on her conflicting identities and initiates a dialogue between them. The aim is to get to know the qualities, wants and needs of each aspect, then to disidentify from them in order to find an objective viewpoint and central sense of self.

Psychosynthesis uses this technique. It also works with imagery which is a medium favoured in Jungian analysis. Through an image, we may access something which is too obscure or unbearable to fully feel within us. Image making keeps us at a safe enough distance from that which we have split off from. For instance, early in therapy, I had an image of a white dragon standing in a kitchen who was puffing out steam while rolling pastry - which, as all cooks know, needs cool handling.

Images, also those in dreams, can evoke strong sensations and emotions. They provide uninhibited material which we may subsequently interpret and expand upon, therefore bring into greater focus, that which is just out of reach in our psyche. *Guided imagery* and affirmations might change our thought patterns so that a different feeling response or action follows. Overlaying what is negative with positive thinking may feed our will. For example, had I been led on to visualise my dragon re-directing steam at some cooking pots on the kitchen stove, this might have subtly influenced how I channelled my power so that it was more effective.

Visualising that we are going up a mountain or into a cave may bring such an altered state of mind that, like taking L.S.D., it opens up our boundaries into both the transpersonal and psychotic dimensions. Thus these directive techniques might sound an ideal way of probing the deep primal wound.

It can be an astounding moment when we fully grasp that our superego has created a persona with exactly the opposite qualities to the ones we keep in our shadow. When we realise the terrible truth that we have the capacity to be all that we have always worked hard to prove that we are not, it may be a painful but also a healing time. Honesty is magnificently freeing. It can be a glorious occasion when we discover the gifts contained in those hitherto repressed parts. The atmosphere becomes almost evangelical. One more soul saved.

All these marvellous emotional insights might come in a self development workshop, so popular in a consumer society which expects a quick fix - our wants, rather than our deeper needs, satisfied. During such enlightening shifts of perception, we may recognise our discredited parts and even identify with a crazy aspect. Everyone feels satisfied. Another successful outcome.

But this sudden realisation is just the beginning of the trail as these shadow aspects are formations or complexes and not the basic properties. What of the primal state before we had any psychic refining ability? Never mind the steam - what about the fire in the belly of my dragon?

Through active imagination I had met my inner white dragon and three years on, it came at me 'for real', now red and rampaging with fiery breath. Recognising that we have a mad part, then dialoguing with it or discharging it into the ether is not enough. The reason for this is that the released energy, both base and transpersonal, has to go through a slow distillation process and, unless humanised, such archetypal elements remain unintegrated.

As with reorganising physical structure in *body work*, we can pretend to be master of our psyche and develop, apparently, strong will and love dynamics through exercising our psychic muscles and reforming our mental functioning. But while this work can bring exciting breakthroughs and can be ostensibly empowering, it is often superficial, as the challenge to substantiate a true intra-psychic relationship through a mature therapist can be avoided.

A therapist who uses proactive methods would have had me translating my hallucinated attacking panther into an assertive power animal and the many torturing implements into tools for extracting my truth. While I might eventually envisage these turn-arounds with good effect, had I recoursed prematurely to such reframing practices, I would have buried the hatchet underground so to speak, rather than contacting the feeling of wanting to bury it in someone else's skull.

When our centre is not true, what comes out of these practices only adds weight to the subpersonalities which surround our adapted self and, like rogue satellites, these can pull us further off our true course. Such devices may free up some constricted aspects but they do not bring lasting freedom.

**

Section B *Discovering what it takes*

The heart of therapy lies in the relationship. For a client, the therapist represents any number of significant others - foremost our primary carers but also siblings, teachers, friends, partners, boss - even god. This transfer of psychic energy, that is the attachment of emotions from another relationship from another place and time onto the therapist, is called *transference*.

The true source of the transference may be totally hidden from us for some time. Indeed, when coming from the depths of our narcissistic wound, the transference may gather such momentum, or already be so strong, that we cannot see any of our therapist's real identity. If extremely regressed to when we were unified in 'mother', we may be under the ultimate delusion that he is the warm or contracting womb, the 'good or bad breast', the comfortable full or painful stomach.

Within the therapeutic container we may vividly replicate our emotional history in what could be deemed as a war zone, a meeting place for souls and everywhere in between. Whether old or recent, remembered or forgotten, our past can be transposed onto the present and becomes our living experience.

While there are always currents and impulses in our surrounding field which affect us, generally these lie below the level of most people's perception. Neither do we notice all visual, auditory and tactile cues and nor could we cope with consciously processing all this extra stimuli when modern life bombards us with so much.

However, while our therapist will have a natural response to elements in our replayed story, he may also draw, from the effects of the combined psychic *field*, the emotions which match those felt by people we imagine him to be. These responses induced by our behaviour and by the affects of our unconscious on the field which are felt by the therapist, are called the *countertransference*.

Impulses and emotions of both therapist and client contribute to, and constellate within, this interactive field. When we cast our therapist as the inadequate part of our original carer, he might find this *negative transference* particularly hard to deal with if he has not thoroughly worked through his own primal attachment issues.

He might even become hostile. Naturally, such emotion will be in the field and just may be an appropriate response. Any retaliation on the therapist's part could, however, indicate that he cannot bear being used as an object since his sense of self is fragile. He will, therefore, be out to defend his ego, instead of coming from a place where he, as therapist, is re-presenting antagonistic elements in the service of us, the client. Rather than holding a clear enough space for us to realise how we automatically fabricate these familiar negative feelings towards us, so that we may change our ways and find our perceptions unfounded, the therapist can actually become an abusive carer.

There again, a therapist might try and quickly repair any discord since he cannot afford to jeopardise his source of confirmation of self as a 'good' carer. Attention from replaying the primary set up can be easily diverted. Rather than coping with the experience of being seen as somebody abusive or bad, he inhibits any challenge which may come from our self emergence by metaphorically, or sometimes literally, stroking us.

While tender loving might seem to be the perfect treatment for one who has had precious little, such compensatory 'caring' can keep our true self immobilised. Heartless as it may sound, often it is best if only meagre rations essential to survival are given to one caught by delusions - otherwise, why seek freedom. Pouring oil on troubled waters is only a short term resolution.

Having an experience of a warm holding environment may be necessary to build a good enough alliance. However, 'making things better' or reasoning challenging emotions away can result in reformation of a fractured psyche. We are seemingly mended but we maintain both the unreality and deformity of the adapted self.

Alternatively, rather than let our therapist manifest as inadequate, we may conceive him to be the ideal mother we never had. In turn, we might try and make ourselves appealing so that he also finds us special. Perhaps we crave to possess him as in a primary identification or, indeed, to act on erotic fantasies. Further still into the psychotic transference, we could start to worship the ground he walks upon as we render ourselves to our therapist who is the archetypal saviour.

While the therapist needs to accept such positive transference, encouraging an imbalanced liaison is disempowering since, in idealising the therapist, the client stays split off from her own true ideal part. A client will swing naturally to the negative transference in due course, given the chance.

I can think of many clinical cases where there has been a two-way massaging of egos. In one, the relationship was as cozy as that of a mutual admiration society. But there was no way out, no chance of the client individuating. Each used the other to get more and more fixes, until the client found heroin as a substitute. If she could not release her aggressive forces and separate from her stand-in-mother, who was 'killing her with kindness', then she could terminate the alliance by killing off herself.

*

As a client, we might easily regress to childlike dependence before we become truly self sufficient. This handing over of power can be an intoxicating trip for a therapist, however. There is great potential to manipulate another's psyche for one's own ends when its workings are understood. Clients are vulnerable prey for any hungry narcissistic predator lying in a therapist's shadow.

Twenty odd years ago I was in an ideal position, as a novice therapist, to nourish my wounds by proxy. As with all therapists, I had taken tentative steps towards peeling away my defensive layers. Like many, I had also felt stirrings from my deep unconscious. I had even encountered the odd psychotic part and then managed to reassemble my adapted self so that my patina of normality and respectability was quickly restored. There are other therapists who have dipped in and out of psychotic material in this way. All are invaluable as they may similarly enable their clients to do the same. However, none will know what it is like for a client when a mad internal world becomes the norm.

Naturally, some therapists will have been blessed with a primary carer who satisfied their narcissistic needs reasonably well; one who enabled them to assimilate their primal energies enough for them to hold these elements for similarly unscathed clients. In such cases, both parties have a sufficiently strong core self so as not to be particularly shaken by any remaining psychotic material and neither would they need to be.

There again, a therapist who is intellectually identified would withstand a client's rising psychotic forces because he is operating from the perspective of mind over matter. This is so - but at what cost. In order to maintain this stronghold, he stays ahead of, rather than with a head, heart and soul alongside, his client.

Suppose that we, as a client, are submerged by psychotic matter. Rather than find, over time, that this can become manageable, a therapist who has only skidded around on the surface of madness may quickly try to decode and superimpose a sane interpretation on top of our psychotic layer.

This tendency to translate, rather than experience jointly, psychotic elements reminds me of a particular moment I shared with a client. She had survived her crazy childhood environment by developing great mental insight, at the expense of her emotions. She trusted my mental exploration with her but not my feeling response. Once, when she was lost in chaos, I took a risk and said that I was not sure what to make of what was going on for her. Although disquieting to learn that I did not have all the answers, she felt that I was beside her in her uncertain world and, as a result, she positively glowed. A client needs to experience what is the reality of the therapist in order for her to know what is true within herself.

But finding exactly the right level of communication with someone who is fragmented is often impossible. When I was extremely wobbly and my therapist's pitch was just a fraction out, the effect was as great as a satellite shooting past its mother spaceship into infinity. You may think that an empathic 'mmh' would be a safe response. But even this can be wildly wrong when we are touching on madness since we feel, not only that we are losing our mind but, also, that we are fizzling out all together. In fact, it is our adapted personality which is falling apart and losing its control on life. But our core self will have felt a similar sense of annihilation way back when primary mirroring and containing failed.

Only when we are able to recreate in the therapeutic field all the turbulent properties which for a fragile infant were too unbearable to manage alone and so were repressed, may the primitive elements be owned and integrated. This is an extremely challenging process which involves a lot of two-way experimentation.

I had to not only learn how to protect myself from 'snapping' and 'cold hearted' father and 'slimy' mother figures, as in my waking dream of reptiles, but to also experience the effect of the same elements within me. The destruction directed at my self, I needed to exhibit to my therapist over and over again for any enduring changes to occur. In this way I came to accept that how I treated my self, and the treatment that I received from others, I was also capable of dishing out.

The accent is on the word 'capable'. While our neanderthal urges may need to let rip in the confines of therapy, the objective is to gradually transform them into what truly serves us and mankind. The therapist who does not reason this flood of impulses away is supporting us in discovering our true mindfulness.

What is potentially life-giving energy may be inhibited by seemingly well meaning interventions. Often this is due to the therapist's fear that the client's psychotic elements will be overwhelming. Rather than the therapist feel mad, he can drive a client ultimately madder in order to maintain a distinctive line between his own psychotic aspects and those of his client. The therapist remains clearly separate and superior. He dissociates.

I remember being in group therapy and speaking quite normally when I was suddenly struck by a flashback. Immediately, the leader said, 'I do wish you wouldn't do that' - just as if she was scolding a recalcitrant child. It was enough to bring on a choking fit, after which, I depersonalised.

We all instinctively sniff out each other's weak points. Any hidden anxiety belonging to the therapist is likely to magnify the naked terror of a client who is being carried away by psychotic matter. Her antennae will be tuned-in to the finest of tremors. Constantly, she will be testing to the limit whether mad elements might be borne by the therapist, and therefore by herself, or whether their discharge will shatter the environment.

According to a military commander, 'The ordinary soldier is reassured and operates better if his officer has "been there", "done that" and it helps if he has had a few bits blown off him.' Although it is rarely appropriate for the therapist to reveal his battle scars, a client will soon sense whether he has survived the full brunt of psychotic forces, therefore can do so again. Such forces may pass through such an experienced intermediary so that resources are pooled.

✷

What matters above all else is a therapist's genuineness; his humanness, including his basest and finest levels, his limitations, mistakes and gifts. When these are honoured within himself, this honesty might support a client in opening and healing the primal wound. The healthy therapeutic way of development is the challenge of making good use of difficulties and it is in this spirit that I highlight here the possible problems in working with primal forces.

We have to start again with all our illusions of inflation and deflation and eventually check out what is going on in the experiential field, if we are to bring some objective reality to magical thinking. The Sufi, Vilayat Khan speaks of this healing process - '*Disinfection. Sometimes we have to re-open wounds. The remedy is Truth.*' and further, 'Illusion breaks on the rock of truth.'

The delusional client needs a therapist who responds to her in a steadfast, authentic way. Through such constancy, she may be able to bear the coming together of extreme and opposing forces in herself and to realise that such intensity does not destroy the relationship - a different outcome to past experience.

Yet this process is such a trial and error affair as the unfolding of self is so unique. Therefore, let it not be forgotten that my suggestions are based on what has worked for me in the therapeutic encounter and so are particularly angled towards clients with a fragile sense of self. (Do not be fooled by the correspondingly tough persona which so often hides this.)

While a therapist who has dared to plunge to the depths and returned will know the drive of the true self to manifest against all odds, particularly those adapted self preservation tactics, he cannot implant in another the will or the wherewithal to similarly come through these realms. I say this as, from my eagerness here, you might deduce that it is I who put a client through the ordeal of psychotic exploration - far from it. My personal experience merely makes room for the possibility, accommodates the client to go there if so drawn, in a relatively safe enough setting.

Indeed, if I was to force or induce a client in this direction, the thrust would come from me, not from inside her, and her embryonic self would 'miscarry' or emerge 'deformed'. Therefore, rather than push a client to this end, I believe that where I come from, the self born through the psychotic realms, may be felt in the subtle field and ease the way.

It was not to be with a client of mine who came prior to my knowing psychosis. From the very first session I had looked at the top of his head. His gaze was either fixed on an electrical socket above the skirting board or on my shoes. Ostensibly, I could not reach anything below his helmet of hair. He was an expert in making me feel what it was like to be locked in his world.

His wife had made several attempts at hanging herself and he certainly was doing his best to psychically kill me off. I was meant to fail him and, sadly, we rarely met across the therapeutic space in any direct way. After a few months, his wife's condition precipitated psychiatric interest in him and so he ended his therapy with me. But, as he stood at my doorway for the last time, he reached out. With tears in his eyes he looked straight at me and said, 'I have never been as close to anyone in my life and probably won't be again.'

This case exemplifies the void, the empty divide between therapist and client which neither can cross when there has been inadequate primary connection. Each is transfixed by the terror of non being because a client also holds up a mirror for the therapist to see himself, or lack of self in this instance. Generally a client may go only as far as the therapist's complexes and defences permit and at the time of our meeting, I had not been to the abyss and found my self.

*

Many clients are impatient to be cured by their therapist and pressurise him into delivering solutions. Thus a therapist might easily recondition a client into a new form which he thinks appropriate - a further adaptation of the undeveloped self. Also, there is great temptation to force along such 'progress' because it can be harrowing to be with a severely depressed client, for example, who has lost the will to live. In an attempt to numb her pain, she will have deadened all sensitivity and she will be withdrawn from the therapist.

A therapist whose true self has come to life through the process of the adapted self 'dying', will know that by staying sufficiently present and long enough with uncertainty and the tension of an impasse, the client's desensitised elements may return naturally into invigorating emotions.

A client with masochistic tendencies who is systematically exterminating herself would try the patience of a saint. But stamping out this powerful urge would inhibit the very energies which need releasing into the boundaried space which therapy offers. Self-destructive behaviour may need to run its course while the mortal therapist endures the effects of such disablement and also resists - maybe occasionally allows - the client's attempt to pull him into serving as her opposing sadist.

What happens intra-psychically to such a client becomes conscious through inter-acting her familiar dynamics with the therapist. Gradually and in a roundabout way, the sado-masochistic forces may be owned and reformed into healthy, complementary qualities of receptivity and assertiveness by the client.

'I'm not going to fire the gun which you hold to your head, when you ask me to', was one of my therapist's comments when I was unconsciously setting up an abusive scenario with him, yet again. After years of using him as a fall guy, he hoped with this graphic metaphor to interrupt my pattern of projecting my annihilating forces onto him. By being unwilling to play this game with me any longer, it could collapse. There I was trying to re-enact a sado-masochistic dynamic but he was challenging the myth that everyone was out to murder me. The power to destroy myself, which I was giving to him, he was returning to me so that I might channel my aggression constructively.

In the past, probably such a retort from him would have wiped me out. Indeed, I was on a hair trigger to fear but, this time, I was a bit quicker on the draw. Certainly I felt caught out but laughed, and then I pointed my finger as if to shoot him. Was it safe enough for both of us to stand firm in our power? He did not waiver, and neither did I on this occasion, and I realised that he was actually holding out a helping hand rather than firing a body blow. He was not my adversary. This moment, when symbolically I fired rather than 'bit the bullet', is one of the many turning points when I dared to try out a totally new course of action. The transference, particularly the basic life/death drive which I had attached to my therapist, was loosening its hold.

It was at a time when I envisaged impending catastrophes everywhere and the very worst scenarios happening - and some did. Thus it took innumerable occasions of 'facing my fear and doing it anyway', in session and out, for me to recognise that not everyone was out to get me. Finding the origin of my projections in the therapy session, the kernel of truth and the fabrications, has been essential for me to recognise what are delusions and what is fact in my life in general.

✻

The principle therapeutic task is to meet, and then to take back, the emotions and thoughts which we have disowned. In order to mobilise what we had to repress in infancy, we need the freedom to make our therapist out to be incompetent, over protective, jealous, narcissistically absorbed, demanding, invasive, angry, shaming - as abusive. We need this because we are seeking reparation of our wound. We are endeavouring to prove that, this time, the inadequate part of our primary carers, or how we experienced them to be, will give us what we crave for.

But rather than break the enigma, by immediately interpreting such transference, it is important that our therapist allows us to experience these 'negative', or wished for, presences which we perceive in him and then over time, to recognise these in our psyche, for our self. Unintegrated drives demand satisfaction; either we turn these inward or we project them onto others. Often, we do both. By experiencing this duality in the field, we may become responsible for our condition. Similarly, in playing out the original echoes from childhood, sincere acceptance and respect on the part of the therapist for our emerging self might be gradually introjected by us.

Since infancy, those of us with a deep narcissistic wound

have hoped that someone will know exactly how we feel, which is why it is essential that we make our therapist have a taste of what it is like to be us. Our inner child can be so desperate to be heard and accepted that we seize every opportunity in a creative container for healing.

Even when we try not to punish our therapist and/or 'love him to death', we say and do the most bizarre things in order to generate his understanding. At a surface level, we may be unaware of how we are reproducing unresolved issues and how we are affecting our therapist. Yet, operating undercover, the seducer or sadist in us may find many cunning and cruel ways of extracting enough evidence that someone knows our most intimate self yet still stays with us. Familiar neurotic tactics, and some new baser devices may become apparent in time.

We can turn round our exacting, internalised parental voice so that it is coming from our therapist, even if he is speaking lovingly to us. We may use the power of our victim to put out our hopelessness and helplessness into the field in order that he will feel ineffective in his therapeutic role. Then to cap it all, he might fall into our trap of getting him to really act like our parents. The ways of manoeuvering are captivating and fascinating.

Those emotions which we, as a client, dare not contact or express, can be replicated within the therapist and then revealed, sometimes explicitly fed back to us, by him. When they come from a pre-verbal time, he will generally feel them at a somatic level. For example, if we are presenting as an inflated narcissist, our therapist might have sensations in his body of contraction or collapse. He will be picking up our primary deflation of self - what we have had to defend ourselves from feeling.

As a therapist, I find that boundaries often seem to blur in such a primary setting. This is hardly surprising as I can represent to the client the 'absent' depressed mother who disappears or the devouring 'witch' and also, the one with whom absolute fusion is longed for but also feared. Sometimes, I have experienced unformed elements from extremely regressed clients filtering out like a mist enveloping a field so that senses coagulate. Little room is left for differentiation and it is hard to see or reflect the tendrils emanating from the primal forces, yet they cling to us both.

Mostly, the fear is that, were these obscured elements to gain resolution and one of us come into full focus, the other will be wiped out - primary versus secondary narcissistic needs. In this milieu, I have discovered that reminding myself of the terror of non being, so dreadful that it must be concealed at all costs, helps to clear some space for the true self to be conceived. In time, the desperate urge to have a genuine interaction with someone might mean that my client begins to own and direct her raw feelings towards me. Through incorporating this truth she begins to feel the edges of her form and to realise that I too have maintained mine. We can come together yet survive separately.

All this to-ing and fro-ing of hidden energy may sound like a masquerade ball. But it can feel more like a dramatic, death defying duel for survival. All the sensations, drives and emotions which neither we nor our primary carer could tolerate, and therefore had to be seemingly obliterated, will be in the field. Once again, what is surfacing might feel unbearable to deal with.

Being with someone in the violent throes of a psychotic episode can be scary. With such antagonistic yet confused forces raging within, there is a tendency to collapse one or other end of the poles rather than stay with the tension of this battle. Yet while the psychotic client might pour forth forcible, manic energies, she may also emit drifts of excruciatingly painful urges and emotions, full of softness and tenderness. The essential goodness in the newborn, which has been harboured in the psychotic layer, has to be handled with great care.

This sacred dance may be both tragic and beautiful, heart breaking and warming. By restaging early dynamics, in different configurations and over many therapy sessions, we might regain the emotions associated with the original loss of self. However, it is touch-and-go as to whether we stay long enough to experience the awfulness of no continuing sense of being so that we come truly to life. Birth is a mucky, painful yet wondrous experience. It is the hardest yet most productive of labours.

∗

Section C A therapeutic rock or rocking

... a deadly longing for the abyss, a longing to drown in [one's] own source, to be sucked down to the realm of the mothers [as in] the gateway to the unconscious, the Eternal Feminine [where] the divine child slumbers, patiently waiting his conscious realisation. (Jung, 1956)

'One day, you will thank me for throwing you back on your own resources' said my therapist as he urged me to to look after myself. But at this point in time, about a year after my first psychotic episode, I was not up to appreciating how his 'tough love' might empower me. Sometimes I hated this man on whom I depended, although it was to be a while before I could acknowledge this to myself, let alone to him. Thus rather than shaking my head in dissent, my whole body shook.

Teetering on the edge of madness is exhausting. There is a longing to surrender; to either give ourselves up to authoritative medics who can ease such torment with psychotropic drugs, which manipulate our mood as our primary carer could, or to give in to the forces which seek to take us over. I spoke of my craving to be tucked up in bed, safe and sound, with a soothing nurse by my side, when being dragged into my psychotic world.

Sometimes, I would crouch for hours wedged into a corner of my kitchen. It was as if the hard walls and cold stone floor held me together. Were I to move, my insides would fall out, of that I was sure. There was no way I could assemble my senses sufficiently even to crawl away to bed. I needed the solidity of stone to give my body an edge so that I knew where I ended and where other-ness began.

But mostly, I wanted to return to the womb and I would lie in the bath for hours. There was nothing more that I could do. The water soothed and supported what felt like my raw substance, while I had Gorecki's haunting 3rd Symphony constantly flowing through the airwaves. The repetitive tones resonated with my own searing vibrations, a reassuring echo of others who had been to the depths of soul endurance – so I was not alone in this.

While I yearned to return to archetypal mother for

gentle rocking, I had found that the after-effects of the angel cradling me in Glastonbury only further disempowered me. The angel clearly fulfilled my wish for comfort and love - the *pleasure principle* - yet this magnified my disturbance. Thereby I came to realise that what I wanted, was not what was needed. The tenderest of physical holding proved to be over-stimulating. I was too raw to be touched and pure love was as antagonistic to me as hate and anger - such can be the concomitant oscillation of opposing life and death impulses in psychosis, the double bind is both source and symptom. Even just a suggestion of someone coming towards me would send spasms through my nervous and muscular systems. I craved for contact, yet I was horrified by it.

As an infant, I was similarly confounded. But it was a sudden, spontaneous memory of abuse when I was five, which seriously disturbed my structure as an adult and spun me down into the primitive realms. Having buried my anger towards the perpetrators of this abuse at the time, the malevolence was being activated by my recollections. But I was still directing it at myself, while I experienced, in any contact, the terror and shame surrounding the original violation.

Everything and everybody seemed too arousing to my hypersensitive form. It was as if my skin had been severely burnt so that my viscera had no protective encasement. Just a whisper, a touch as light as a feather or even gentle warmth can feel too stimulating to one whose substance is so frail.

Naturally my torment also aroused discomfort in others. Around my tender border gathered a chain reaction of 'touchy feely' affection which brought out the 'huggy' brigade. While I shrank from such effusive advances, it was ages before I could say 'No', directly, to these people who were reaching out ostensibly to help me.

For the most part, they were seeking reassurance for themselves. At a sensory level I knew this because what I found was that my nerve endings were gradually able to adjust to a loving hand which was 'just there' to hold, if I could, whereas an outstretched hand felt demanding and penetrative - few grasped the difference although I tried hard to explain. Even what later I might recognise as a well intentioned act felt dangerous and so, for the most part, I struggled on alone.

My fear of touch, even more so of restraint and therefore of being sectioned to a psychiatric ward, actually turned to my advantage in that I fought hard to contain my inner demons, particularly in public. I had just enough awareness to realise that I could not afford to draw attention to myself and that I must maintain some semblance of form with others – although my son and daughter later told me that they had considered calling 'the men in white coats to take me away'. By wrestling with what was gripping me, for the most part by myself, I was forced to face what I lacked and to find what really sustained me.

*

I suffered a lot before I accepted that my shaking body was not only a sign of fear but was also coupled with fury. Fury was rocketing up inside me, but finding no target, it kept returning to blast me out of existence. As a child, any hostile emotion had been forbidden absolutely and so stayed stored in my body tissues. Fury had no apparent means of expression until, in the space of a week, I found that my canine teeth were no longer pointed but flat. My once chattering teeth were now furiously grinding away under the cover of sleep – a welcome conversion of my hallucinated sabre-toothed panther.

Gradually, it was registering that, without a doubt, I had a very hurt, occluded part of me who – and this was as vast and primal as it can get when it first burst forth – who really wanted to exterminate other people in return. No wonder I had stifled my urge to sincerely engage with the world and had tried to rise above it. Underneath it all, I was as terrified of releasing what was in me as I was of the same coming towards me.

Rather than literally ripping others to shreds, when the rest of the world was asleep, my fingers would instead tear across sheets of paper, fury dictating horrendous utterings against my abusers. Writing it down stopped my fists from pounding my body in an attempt to avert its awful unmanageable impulses. Sensations rose in crescendo, or terror took its hold and I fell into abject submission. My rage pushed for more outlets so then I vented into a tape recorder dark venomous bile which had coagulated with blood from my wounds. I did not know this was inside me. It was so good to spew forth this muck and even better to hear myself doing it. But it was never enough.

Such was the impact of the tumultuous forces, from within and without, past and present, that every frayed nerve and body tissue was excruciatingly alive. The constant neural firings were like electrical charges surging through me and the ongoing climactic sensations meant that my body seemed perpetually on the edge of exploding.

After two years of suffering this awful visceral pressure, a suggestion was that I might get relief if I 'let myself go' in an actual physical container. So I went to a rehabilitation centre for the mentally ill where there was a padded room. Ironically, it turned out to be a surreal pleasure dome for stimulating the senses of those who were severely shut down - the very antithesis of what I craved. But knowing my body as I do now, I suspect that I would have dissolved still further in a padded cell rather than find any long-term relief.

As it was, I continued to bear the nerve racking sensations for several years until gradually, I came to decipher and respond to my body's signals of alarm and, in turn, I found that they began to quieten. But it took many years of painstaking therapy before I could move towards another, or allow anyone to come close to me, without feeling shock waves surging through my body.

Throughout this time, my therapist alternated between metaphorically applying firm pressure to stem my flow of psychotic energy and releasing his hold. He likened this therapeutic technique to the medical procedure of using a tourniquet to stem blood which is flowing from a cut artery and how inhibition must be followed by periodic release.

This is the maxim for the experience of psychosis to be a creative endeavour. It is imperative for psychotic elements to pump out, as well as to be clamped, not just for sanity's sake but because they are the essential raw ingredients of the strong true self. Thus I learned, by example, to manage this movement for myself and to take possession of these vital, once forbidden, forces.

Had my therapist been a dispenser of soothing therapy or sublimating medicament it would have been a different story. The alternative option would have been for these primal forces to forever possess me or to find an external medium which could take control of them for me. While drugs dull the painful symptoms, like rescuing therapists, ironically, they often induce a rocking motion in the patient which assuages, temporarily, the longing for comfort and peace. Redfearn (in Samuels, 1989) lists many countertransferential impulses including those of rocking the deprived client.

Being present with someone suffering the horrors of full-blown delusions can be unnerving and there are no hard and fast rules. The primal wound of the psychotic client is already fully exposed like a cancerous growth which has burst forth its seething, self-attacking mass. Whether there are forceful or insidious emanations of the instinctual forces, effecting the right amount of cohesion of the broken down boundaries in the psychotic field is exacting. Ideally, the therapeutic container will be sufficiently permeable for an osmotic movement of this material.

*

I would ramble incoherently about the terrible things going on for me, presuming that, somehow, my therapist was with me in this mayhem and therefore he could make sense of it. But rather than strive to follow the exact content of what I was pouring forth, it was more important that my therapist stay with the sensations and emotions which were impacting on him - often what I was not in touch with and so was not saying. His task was to hold the potential of what was emerging, what I had the making of becoming.

Whatever triggered my disappearance into my crazy realm also needed to be recognised and worked with. The contents had to be linked with the context in which I was playing out my experiences. Mostly, I was the infant who did not know about 'me' and 'not-me'. Correspondingly, attention needed to be paid to how I came back to some semblance of self, which also would bring me an awareness of my therapist in his own right. He was not really a member of my family, a partner, enemy or hallucinated entity. He was not the one who wanted to exterminate me, even if I tried to make him feel like it.

Despite sounding prescriptive, the movement was truly organic as we both needed to switch back and forth in order to form some ties with the rock of reality. But being caught between two worlds is mind-blowing. Therefore, my tendency was to use all my might to keep each at bay as, when they collided, I could not trust any of my perceptions. Even a threatening reality is better than none at all and we will fight, using any means, rather than go near a nihilistic state. I was lost in my fluctuating world in which projected and internal force fields clashed. The field was full to overflowing with the urge for annihilation - the death wish. There was such fluidity of energy, often we came close to mutual possession.

Just as I was engulfed in turmoil, so I was swamping my therapist and, occasionally, he brought this dynamic to a head. He was tightening the tourniquet. A couple of times he said, 'I'm not inside your head', or, 'I'm not a mind reader.' Such reminders always surprised me since what was inside, to me, felt as though it was outside and vice versa. This straight talk cut incisively through my addled brain, snapping me back into relatively ordinary reality like a slap on my face from a wet flannel. But normally, coming round after a bout with my psychotic entities was a slow, erratic motion.

After my therapy session a room would be found where I was to gather enough strength, gain enough balance to leave the clinic and get myself home. Hovering on the threshold between madness and some sense of sanity is tortuous. In this liminal place, psychic and body boundaries twist and turn. I could not be sure of what was fact or fantasy – the edges were blurred. Yet my task was set and always the same. I would go through a lengthy process of trying to focus on the solid objects around me, while forcing back the psychotic drag to turn them into monsters.

But to begin with, there was nothing firm in my mind's

eye. Neither was there anything stable to hold onto, not even the chair I sat on, nor could I ground myself by feeling my feet on the floor. It felt like I was trying to straddle two bolting horses which were intent on going in opposite directions. I had taken leave of my senses and they had taken possession of me. To my ears, nearby sounds meant predators closing in on me and it seemed ages before I could tune into a clearer wavelength so these became recognisable voices which were just filtering up from the clinic below. What was outside could only be let in ever so gradually, for my perceptions to mingle in any safety.

But despite taking this time following a session, the shock of physically stepping through the front door into the big wide world always sent me reeling. The space between the clinic and my parked car seemed like a killing ground and I clung to any intervening walls and trees in an attempt to hide and steady myself. Hooded parking meters threw living shadows which, to me, were masked thugs waiting to mash my brain into a pulp. I saw vultures instead of sparrows. I could not tell whether what passed me by inhabited my inner or outer world. I did not really know where I was.

Where there is an upheaval of deep psychic matter, the ground opens up and we can fall into the bowels of madness. Everything can change dramatically from moment to moment. What is normally invisible to the naked eye is larger than life and what is ordinarily obvious, diminishes into obscurity.

Of course, the pull of opposing forces in a more normal mental state insists that we practice taking flexible attitudes, extruding into different shapes as we identify and disidentify with the many and various aspects without and within.

But when our image-making ability runs amok, such fabrications may become so embedded as autonomous entities that they have the power to dictate what we do and feel. They may originate from our ancestors, or be extreme archetypal figures or 're-presentations' of our primary carers. Yet while relating to these imagined entities as ghosts from our past, we also need to treat them as missing and disconnected aspects of our self which continue to blitz us. In this way, rather than be personifications out there, they may become personalised and integrated.

Instead of exorcising my demons, and my overpowering angels for that matter, I had to get to know these disguised energies which had been buried under years of fear. They could empower me. I needed to turn and meet my self in the terror of my hitherto forbidden, and therefore obscure, assailants. But while I needed to let go of the total belief in my delusions, I had to decipher their messages, as they held an important significance that was part of my history.

Over time, I saw how my hallucinations could help in illuminating the core of my wound. They were not reality but a meaningful metaphor. With this realisation, which only came to me in snatches, these manifestations lost some of their destructive power and gradually became a medium of creative reasoning. I might have been crazy but there was some method in my madness after all. Out of the bones of the spectres of my past, I was to build a new psychic structure.

*

When verging on madness, there is always the danger that we can remain passively tied as a victim to our primal forces. In this way we have an identifiable world, even if it is a highly distorted one.

If we are to avoid psychotic manifestations becoming firmly established, without taking desensitising drugs, we need someone to hold us in our initial dissemination. This should not be in such a way that our condition is prematurely 'cured' and our response determined for us. Generally, the truth of our past, present and potential future can only gradually be revealed by us and then carefully to us. Rather, we need the grasp of a firm hand in a soft glove in order to stay with the uncertainty of the chaotic forces.

While on the planet of psychosis, we inhabit regions where ordinary reason ceases to function. Here we might make rules and codes in a language all of our own. When a therapist can hold our truth and our attempt at logic, using his own primary process of intuition, in this outwardly seemingly crazy dimension, together we might find the passwords which will take us through the formations of self. Both parties have to use all the means at their disposal in this process, as we ride with psychosis on a wing and a prayer.

In this mutuality, terror might dissipate and the fierce driving forces lose some of their charge so that we start to express recognisable emotions, however thoughtless, unpolished and foolish they might sound to begin with. What starts as a mass of teeming energy storming through us can transform into more conscious and manageable feeling states as we take over our therapist's mediating and containing role.

Some three years after madness had blasted through my defences and was tempering out a little, I had a vision of a donkey whose head and body were held fast in a brace. Its life was of torture and utter despair. It could only endure the cacophony of sound, the piercing strobe lights which surrounded it and the electrical charges which shot up through the floor. My body felt these forces and heaving sobs came up like brays, as I sucked in and bellowed out air. The phenomenon is still extraordinary when I come to think of it now.

But rather than being in a full-blown hallucination, I was imagining myself in an identifiable form at last, however lowly and dumb. I was beginning to objectify myself and see the miserable condition that a subjugated part of me had taken on in life.

Another year passed and the image returned. But I noticed that now the brace around the donkey's head was loosening. I even envisaged a time ahead when the music and lights were no longer discharging their shocking waves. Not only did I interpret this change as evidence that my neural impulses were transforming, but I felt vibrant energy spreading purposefully within me and saw myself moving, albeit tentatively, onto the floor and beginning to dance.

Most significantly, what I pictured had a frame which proved that I was internalising some of my therapist's psychic holding. I was forming some mental constructs in which to organise and incorporate what was trying to possess me, those cataclysmic elements which were really mine. With this perspective in mind, I could begin to disidentify from my debasement.

No one else could make these choices for me or provide the will to wrestle with my overbearing forces. Having unleashed the furies, I alone was responsible for pulling my self together. Yet being able to respond to, and take responsibility for our self will be a totally new ball game, one difficult to master, when self will has been abnegated in the early formative years.

**

Section D Hitting rock bottom

After five long months of madness, I was starting to lift my head up above the thundering waves of energy, which had dredged up so much emotional debris, and to batten down my hatches, so to speak. I was still floundering but my therapist stood, for me, like a lighthouse, his beacon serving both as a warning and welcoming signal. (These analogies come from when, as a teenager, I spent a terrifying night on a sailing boat caught between two rip tides at the mouth of a Norfolk estuary.)

Now the volume and force of energy which encompassed me seemed as great as a hurricane at sea and this collided with the waves which washed back from my therapist's rock like harbour. Yet the struggle to meet in this maelstrom afforded brief moments when I beheld how my internal world obliterated all else. There is nothing like looking into the eye of a storm to ultimately bring life into sharp focus.

As a teenager, I eventually picked out a torchlight coming from shore which indicated the passageway to safety. And now my therapist was shining a light into my eyes which, once in a while, cleared a new sight line home. I was coming from Neptune's underworld into a more concrete 'here and now'. I fought in earnest to draw these worlds together and for a few weeks my psychosis began to abate.

Here, I need to reiterate my deep-rooted conviction that, had I remained within the relative safety of my therapist's container, I would have managed to maintain this momentum.

Madness, therefore, would not have bedevilled me for so long and my sense of self would have developed from this point onwards.

But as fate would have it, just when I was beginning to form a tenuous hold on reality, I was to meet with a trainer in psycho-physical therapy. Since he was much feted in this field, I had great expectations that he would help placate my body's chaotic energies. I was sorely in need.

Instead, he took me even further into the fathomless depths, from where few return. It really was touch-and-go. I was put through, and must have been mad to submit to, a terrible ordeal at the hands of this teacher. No doubt he wished me no harm. His focus, however, was elsewhere, for he was intent on demonstrating his power and the potency of body work to an audience. This is how it seemed to me.

He had seduced the group with his shamanistic mastery. But I was transfixed and spoke of his words as rarefied vibrations from the collective unconscious which I was hearing through the pores of my skin. He was channelling. We were all under his spell but I was already so open, I was like jelly in his hands. I had asked for gentle support in bringing my body back together. My scream, 'Don't touch me!', either fell on deaf ears or must have determined, maybe excited, him into supposing that invasive touch was exactly what I needed. But he was good and his suggestion that I choose a friend, someone I trusted to help hold me in this work, reassured me. So I did as I was told.

Prolonged and deep pressure by his hands on my body brought excruciating and feverish sensations. It is hard to convey what this was like for me. It elicited the wildest of emotions and I felt once again in the hallucinated snake pit, since not only did my flesh crawl but my pelvic contents were writhing in agony as if creatures were eating my innards. What is so galling to concede is that while these sensations paralleled recent psychotic experiences, this time they were actually being inflicted by a human hand.

The display he performed with me, which seemed to correspond also to some childhood assaults on my being, accorded him much applause. It was mooted subsequently, that this experience was 'good for me' - the message I had heard often as a child. But the proof of this monstrous debacle was in the 'pudding', which was all that was left of me after his handiwork. I had sunk to a subsistence level, gone beyond the normal nadir of life and any shred of will I had left was slipping away from me. Only the finest strand held me to life.

This protracted episode was the culmination of three days of aggressive body work which had dragged me inexorably towards total destruction. Why should I submit to such forceful treatment, you might well ask. Surely I was deranged. But the fact that I allowed such mortification in the hope that it would indeed, do me good, indicated how I had been conditioned as a child. Mother knows best.

*

While the balance of power needs to be held by the therapist, the encounter is dangerous when this power is sustaining a therapist's grandiose self. There is a fine line between allowing the original dynamic between primary carer and child to develop, with awareness, and re-enacting traumatic events in such an all encompassing way which is not at all productive. Such heavy handed work retraumatises a client. The responsibility for recognising the difference, however, lies mainly with the therapist, not with the client.

A therapist may only deduce from the countertransference, his professional experience, supervision and personal therapy, when regression into a familiar pattern is continuing to serve his client and when progression into realising a different response is indicated. It could be that the client's superego has reigned supreme for far too long on the therapeutic stage. On the other hand, it might be that some unconscious aspect in the therapist is leading the field.

Our *wise being, daimon* or soul guide, can be deemed to know what we need to do and experience. There is great truth in this. But it can be an easy way out for a therapist to maintain that he is trusting in the wisdom of a client's psyche, so that he lets all the responsibility for what happens fall on his client.

The best way of minimising the risk of being the recipient and/or the perpetrator of abusive power is to integrate the primal forces. Just as there was an imbalance in the primary relationship, it is essential that this is felt and addressed repeatedly in the therapeutic encounter – but not exploited.

Although it was flashbacks from childhood which precipitated my psychotic episodes back in the summer months, these had then been reinforced in the autumn during an experiential training on Grof's (1985) stages of birth, which an over zealous trainer had encouraged me to take. Through the winter months, however, I was beginning to stabilise. Then I turned to the body worker for support.

But rather than evoking my will by redirecting my imploding rage towards protecting myself, as I feignly hoped, this latest invasive work was further crushing and extinguishing my life force. Instead of engendering some rock-like centrality, it felt as if I was being dashed upon the rocks and rendered senseless.

Following this demolition of my form, there was no grounding of the material produced. After the pounding techniques, came a merging and a complete loss of any substance. He literally rocked me in his arms and I flowed into dark pools as he gazed into my eyes. But I found no oceanic bliss - it was more like a drowning.

I will never forget the sensation of finding a hair in my mouth after this cradling. Like a newborn baby, my tongue explored each crevice and fold in my mouth and I became totally lost in this experience. When someone tidied me up, washed my face of snot and pulled my hair away from my face, I felt utterly bereft. But no one seemed to know how devastatingly empty and terrified this made me feel. I stayed crumpled on the floor for what seemed like an eternity.

The previous night, as a result of similar practices, I had fallen headlong onto the floor. I had feinted and had to be carried to a car to take me home. However, at the end of this most punishing final day, it felt like I was parcelled up, transported and left for dead in my house - and of course, there I lay alone.

When dawn filtered through into my consciousness,

with it came the searing sensations of having had instruments of torture used on my body and probes rammed through my orifices. In fact, keening wails which had lain inside me since my early years, the likes of which I had only heard coming from animals being butchered, had been forced from my insides to the outside and had damaged internal, delicate membranes. My tubes and chambers were so bruised, it pained me to breathe, eat and excrete. I felt completely pulverised.

The days and nights which immediately followed this treatment passed without sleep. Instead I kept slipping into a fugued state while the contents of my house hovered around me seemingly as weightless as I was. I was in no man's land.

*

While the horror of extreme suffering needs to be exposed so that it might effect change, too much at once can mean that we cut off from such stimulation and our conscious mind. This, perhaps, is such a point, so let us take a step forward.

Much of what passed in the following days remains lost to me as other more diffuse energies closed in on me, like dark snakes of smoke curling from the psychotic inferno, which smothered all thought processes. Although difficult to press on here as I write, as it was hard back then to shake off my shroud of silence, I can recall telephoning the clinic where I worked. I was so relieved that the receptionist who answered my call assumed from my hoarse voice that I was suffering from a cold and so, without question, promised to cancel my sessions. I was too 'out of it' to explain what was wrong. Neither could I ask for help. Besides, I could not envisage a form this might take which I could bear.

Having survived some critical time in this petrified nether state, I began to come round to the land of the living, enough to ask my son to collect my car which was still parked close to the scene of the crime. There he found it – its windows smashed, seat belts ripped by flying glass and a lovely big blanket, which I had forgotten to take into college, stolen. I had felt so safe in my car yet it suffered a similar fate to me.

My son has since assured me that, when he brought my car back, he approached me with great care. Yet as he crossed the threshold of my home, it felt as though a tornado had rushed through the door. I was blown away by his force-field. Any introduction to a presence from the dense world can come as a shock when stranded in a raw and rarefied limbo state.

My son then enlisted the help of my daughter. The day that I took with her what felt like my first steps into the broad daylight world, remains imprinted on my mind. She supported me into her car, then into the supermarket where she propped me up against a wire trolley and in my enfeebled state, I clung onto this means of protection and propulsion. It helped me jack up my legs and my resolve, like an invalid with a walking frame.

Of course, I would have preferred to be bundled up and pushed around in the trolley. But my daughter knew instinctively that I needed firm, albeit gentle, encouragement to bring me back into the ordinary world – and food shopping is about as mundane and fundamental as it gets. Although it hurt me, we giggled together over my choice of foodstuffs – apple puree, milky puds and tinned spaghetti were what I craved. Such fare was comforting. This 'baby food' helped to fill the sore holes in my body and I took pleasure in its textures, tastes and smells. I remember the delight of rolling mashed banana and condensed milk around my mouth, of these *play space* moments which were not allowed in infancy.

Even later, when I returned to college the following year, at lunch breaks I would feast on egg mayonnaise sandwiches and hot milky chocolate. I was revisiting my oral phase, growing into my impoverished body and forming a skin. But this time round, I was better able to look after myself and to find the real stuff I was made of.

∗

My fragile hold on sanity had been almost wrenched away by the charismatic teacher. While in this state of invalidity, in both senses of the word, the urge to give up the ghost was strong. Figuratively speaking, I was all at sea. No more was I trembling on the brink of madness. The shoreline had disappeared since I had been pitched over the horizon's rim of normal reasoning.

As a child, I was often taken to the Isle of Wight and in crossing from England's mainland I would hang my beloved teddy bear over the side of the ferry, forever fighting the pull to drop it into the foam. Now, in the wake of my submersion, with my map of reference and network of controls dissolved, there dribbled a vague sense that, if I was to stay afloat, there was no alternative but to alter the course which I had been following since childhood.

The element of water has long been associated with the flow of life. This can freeze when we are cut off from our feelings and we withdraw from what seems like an unwelcoming environment. Our fear is that, were our feelings to melt, they would spill over and flood us. In solution we are held in the womb. Water is symbolic of the newborn and of elementary emotions.

Again, my analogy comes from real life - this time of being up an African creek marooned in a small boat and, as far as the eye could see, surrounded by swarms of jelly fish which had choked the propellor. As then so now, my change in direction was to be more like the slow manoeuvres involved when recovering a broken down craft. Having hit rock bottom, salvaging the wreck, which was all that was left of me after such disabling body work, took an incredible amount of dedicated, painstaking work. There was no one at my helm and I was sinking fast. Water was over the Plimsoll line. So on reflection, I was drifting more like the swarms of jelly fish which were just moving with the ebb and flow of the swell.

However, my therapist cast a delicate supporting net around my amorphous mass. I had reached the end of the line but he held fast this connection. He buoyed me up, enough for me to surface occasionally and take in small gasps of air. Yet I felt no rhyme or reason. I could only just bear my body's instinctual impulses and the currents flowing within; the momentum of which I hoped, with the winds of change, might eventually steer me into calmer emotional waters.

So it came to be, having been saturated by a dark sea of

dread, the seascape of psychic waters was yet to bear me. The tide had its neap and spring phases but was to turn slowly but surely.

But if I was to recover, maybe even to flourish, no longer could I afford to attract and accept such violating forces from without. There were no two ways about it, I had to own and integrate the same forces which lay within. Come hell or highwater, I could not be a slave to my primal forces. I must rule the waves.

To complete the analogy with water, my individuation has come through both tightening the life-line attached to my anchor, the rock of therapy, while I trod water, and letting it out until I could sail a true course on my unfolding sea of energy. There was a continual moving back and forth in fusion and separation.

*

Touch is our earliest language, and therefore, capable of taking us back instantaneously to our most primitive universe. (Conger, 1994)

Our resistance is in the boundary of our body and nowhere is this more concretely felt than with its outer covering, our skin. While a therapist's physical contact might provide an edge, and so foster a sense of 'otherness' and separation, it can equally overlap the border between unity and annihilation. The collective verdict on the efficacy of incorporating body work in psychotherapy is heavily divided and I am still too inflamed by the insults to my body to formulate a sufficiently objective view on this issue. A list of books, therefore, can be found in the bibliography under 'General Reading' for Chapters 5 Section B and 7 Section D, which, in my opinion, present a sensitive approach to accessing emotions through physical touch.

What I would advise, however, is for extreme caution in using psycho-physical therapy, particularly for those whose physical boundaries were transgressed in childhood. Having been conditioned to accept any amount of contact, such a client is easily lulled into a false sense of security and the therapist's touch can compound the damage. Ignoring this liability is iniquitous and therapists should mark Conger's (Ibid) words - *Unfortunately many of us growing up have been so seriously traumatized that our boundary awareness is flawed. As clients we do not know how to protect ourselves against intrusion. We may invite the abuse we suffered in childhood.*

Such was my experience, and there were many bystanders who chose not to see what was really going on for me. A few witnesses came forward afterwards and remonstrated, as I did some years later when I felt strong enough to challenge the effectiveness of such body work. Despite further catastrophes occurring at the hands of this trainer, people continued to clap their hands as he produced such a spectacular display. But to me, he was not sufficiently grounded to be in touch with the true essence of my soul which, in his hands, was trying to embody more fully.

Moving on some four years later, as I had progressed so I was to meet a psycho-physical therapist who had also witnessed, and felt for herself, how destructive this type of work could be. She had decided, therefore, to follow her own way and use more subtle art forms in healing the psyche-soma.

It was at a time when I still felt quite paranoid in a group of people, enough for me to shrink from close encounters and certainly recoil with touch. I was edgy, hyper vigilant, super aware of anyone approaching and nervous of being taken by surprise from behind. I would position myself therefore, either against a wall or get a friend to guard my back. Using these strategies, I could just about cope in communal situations, as generally it was now only in the confines of my therapy session or at home that the embers of madness would flare up.

Thus this trainer did not approach me but waited for the time when I sought to come to her. Her senses seemed finally attuned to mine. She balanced the movement from psyche to soma like a dexterous artist who held the frame, canvas, tools of application and pigments in mind. Even still, it took many proverbial steps forward and back, before I dared to venture physically towards her. Despite the natural blips in this intricate, graphic emergence into a new world order, eventually I nestled into her arms. But I was a bundle of nerves. I still have the minute, exquisite sea shell this therapist gave me after our first real meeting, as a containing symbol of our delicate movements together.

Psychically holding one who has dissolved into a pulp takes the tenderest of care. But touch can feel like a branding iron when we are, metaphorically speaking, skinless. We long for enfoldment but like a fragile moth cupped in warm hands, such contact burns. The slightest 'wrong' move and terror, rage and searing anguish overwhelms like wildfire and takes us further into meltdown mode.

The psychotic transference has to be handled with great sensitivity for it to be resolved. It is hard enough for the infant to form a healthy connection with his primary carer and he is starting from a relatively clean slate. An adult however, who is regressed to this early state, is reliving the difficulties in his primary relationship as well as subsequent failures in affiliation.

*

Therapy might be the first opportunity for us to taste a truly intimate meeting with another human being, if we had a problem with attachment when young. For this *I-Thou* (Buber, 1958) relationship to prosper, there needs to be sufficient two way trust, respect and love for the autonomy of both parties. Building an authentic connection may be a mutually profound process.

When I think of how this special relationship developed between my therapist and my self, the process seems too fulsome to share in any detail, but I may convey its manner and tenor. It often came in moments of stillness when the presence of self could be felt quite clearly. So much happened on a subliminal level which only later was put into words. Yet even when thoughts and feelings were formulated, they seemed inadequate in conveying just how delicate and awesome the tender holding was which nurtured me into being reborn.

The fine movements in such transitions often developed in bittersweet moments when we were lost for words, such was the wonder and terrible depth of emotion in the field. Sometimes, when we came close together everything fell apart. I stole a rare glance and then flipped into the shame of neediness. I felt his warmth and this terrified me, yet I yearned for it. We met at a place which was so new to me.

In everyone's life, at some time, our inner fire goes out. It is then burst into flame by an encounter with another human being.

(Albert Schweitzer)

In all this, I came to learn that truly meeting someone feels completely different to merging with them - in that the sense of self is not lost, snuffed out, but validated. Each time we glimpse the potential in this new way of being, the longing to fully experience it becomes a little stronger and begins to offset the old fear of abandonment and rejection which once prevented self emergence.

Indeed, when the time came for me to move on and work with a female analyst, I found that the love which we had shared lived on in my self. It is through our therapist's sincere and congruent response to us that we might gain emotional access to our authentic self. Having revived and expressed what lies at the base of the psyche, the more we may then safely develop truly intimate relationships full of passion and compassion in the outside world.

The contrast might be so great that the anguish of knowing what we have missed for so many years is hard to bear. But through such poignant experience, not only may genuine intimacy become all the more precious, but so might life on all its different and practical levels. After all, along with the search for self realisation, we are here on earth to really savour life.

In staying unhappy by remembering the past or fearing the future, we forgo contentment and joy in the present (the word 'present' is so named because the living moment is a gift). Having embraced our elemental material, we may discover an innocence, a trust formed through self belief which frees us to play with gusto. Such inclusivity makes for a happy and whole human being.

In the next chapter, therefore, we discuss what it means to enjoy a powerful loving self. From here it can only be a case of onwards and upwards.

✻

Chapter 8

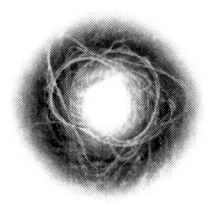

A Centre of Powerful Loving

You have to love your self in order to truly love another. This sentiment is often so glibly said that it is a sickly platitude, just as 'finding our self' has become a cliché. Sadly, the idea of finding and loving our self can produce such an uncomfortable response that its truthful profundity is trivialised. Let us counterbalance this here.

If we love our self, we will want, and have the resources, to look after our self. It seems sod's law that people who had really good loving as children, continue to find it there for the taking and making as adults, whereas youngsters deprived of true love cannot recognise it and so disregard it when older.

When young, we love spontaneously and because we are very needy. We may find, however, that we are only loved when we are loving. If conditioned to love others over and above our self, love may emerge in forceful and subversive ways. Having been loved for what we could give as a child, we may continue to seek love through giving. But love is not real, not a gift but a bargain, when the principal concern is, 'What's in it for us?' Where obligation and coercion are instigators in the art of loving, love will be tinged with bitterness. The so-called milk of human kindness becomes soured by resentment.

Yet unconditional, agape or altruistic love are not synonymous with self sacrifice. Indeed, we can subtly control others under the guise of a loving selflessness – a particularly hollow token if we do not know or value our true self.

Repeating the mantras, 'I love myself' and, 'I am a powerful human being', while standing in front of a mirror, is a common recommendation for curing low self esteem. Acting 'as if' and using hypnotic suggestion to overlay a negative state when there is no true sense of self, reminds me of a budgie who sits in his cage reciting how pretty he is. He is a mere imitation of his natural self.

Through such canting, we might feel flushed for a while. But like Narcissus, who fell in love with his reflection in a pool, we will forever seek reassuring affirmations to sustain this image of our form as, when we kiss the surface of the water, we ruffle this perfect reflection and it disappears. Unless we see in the ripples our neurotic distortions and then dare to look at the bottom of the pool, to the psychotic depths, we may never embrace the substance which makes us who we truly are - neither may others see us clearly or we them.

Remaining blind or indifferent to how love is bound up with neediness, domination, lust, hate and idealisation is not healthy. Until we have integrated those emotions beneath our desires, we lack the capacity for genuine and loving intimacy.

*

Who looks outside dreams. Who looks inside wakes. (popularly attributed to Jung but origin unknown)

Earning love for my adapted self had left me with such a passionate hunger that I had no option but to go within to discover who I was. It was like losing an appetite for adulterated fast food. I only appreciated what I was missing when I had nothing else to ruminate on but my raw ingredients. Although hard to digest, this natural produce eventually proved to be the perfect wholefood for fully filling my self. I could not find what I needed from outside so I had nowhere else to go.

But mine was such rude awakening. For the most part, gone was the cover I had used to fit into a conventional life and, with it, the capacity to communicate in any rational form. Instead, the urge to rattle people's cages was strong. I wanted to wake everyone else up, to let rip with that black panther of mine. With my true self still in its raw embryonic stage, these were dangerous times. I had to withdraw.

Away from others there was space for the fuse of my explosive forces to lengthen, quiet for persecutory elements to still and time for reflection. Here strands of thought and emotion could percolate through the mesh of psychosis so that all might transform into vigorous and tender feelings.

By feeling my abject aloneness, a new found compassion for my past loss and suffering was to emerge which would enable me to take care of my self in the way I should have been as a child.

All alone I didn't like the feeling
All alone I sat and cried
All alone I had to find some meaning
In the centre of the pain I felt inside ...
All alone I came into this world
All alone I will someday die ...
All alone I heal this heart of sorrow
All alone I heal this child ...   (Beth Nielsen Chapman, 1997)

In going into exile, we may find a quiet sense of implicit loving strength growing within. We become genuinely self affirming and at ease by our self. What in us we were taught to dislike, fear, be ashamed of and so occluded, may feel not so bad after all. In fact, we might even come to like our self. Having made a spacious loving room for our self out of the deepest pit in our shadow, from here, we may find a new way back into humanity - with a firm yet sensitive regard for our inherent nature, which others may also respect.

The wonder is that, after a period of adjustment following a psychotic breakdown, truer harmony may flow around us. It seems that our magnetic field alters, clearing the air so that ripples of healing energy affect those even further afield. A genuine and deeply satisfying relationship with our entire being can form which attracts people who mirror back the same. When we are not afraid to show our self and speak our truth, the veils of illusion lift revealing others of the same ilk who do not reject us, even if at times they disagree with what we say or do.

Ultimately, by building up a tolerance within our psychic organisation, we can better manage our responses to people with contrary opinions to our own. Just think about it. Why should we be able to resolve our differences with others if we cannot sort out our own inner dichotomies? If we are secure in our identity, instead of being deflated, defensive or dogmatic, we can be more open to what others have to offer us.

Building real self confidence in this way means we do not have to pretend that we are better or worse than anyone else. When we can accept our limitations and strengths, we have nothing to lose - and that is so freeing. Certainly no amount of condemnation and rejection can invalidate how good it feels to be relieved of the tension from holding back on all that we are.

I was never made of 'sugar and spice and all things nice' - I knew that already. But since my baser nature was exposed in madness, my unpleasantness is more obvious. Similarly, I feel all the more genuine when being pleasant. I also have glimpsed where true tolerance, nobility and graciousness flows.

When we own our imperfect, and purest, powerful and loving ways, we no longer need to idealise or demean others. Dignity and love flow two ways. The joy is that in caring for our primal wound it may become less demanding and significant, therefore we can afford to be more magnanimous. Such is the power of love at the roots of our being.

I subscribe and hearken to this potential within me. All this can happen as I have seen and felt enough to know it deep in my heart. But in the fullness of time because, while I present these ideals, the traumatised child who left her body can only slowly come to life.

*

Awful as the risk of alienation from people might be, separation from who we essentially are is a living death. Maybe we always had a niggling feeling that something was wrong, that we were cheating on our self. But it might not be until we come from our true being that such incongruence is felt as abhorrent. Thus we uphold our once abnegated self, honour what we hold most dear.

Embracing our loving power is an awesome challenge, if this was never duly recognised by our carers. Everything we have been led to believe of ourselves gets contradicted. Not only are we subject to our superego trying to drag us back to our adapted self, but also, in our quest for a fulsome self, others may denounce us as selfish, sad and perhaps mad. Staying small, meek and mild is so often deemed a virtue while loving our magnificence, to be a vice.

Thus, when established ways and belief systems no longer seem to be working or satisfying, many look for a substitute master who can instill a different programme. It is a chilling thought how we might offer our self up to a stranger in exchange for the possibility of deliverance. We 'follow the leader', as in childhood, so that our disparate energies are further hidden in fanatical sects through rapture or force. In our wish to forego the exacting task of taking charge of our driving forces, we can be readily duped in such a master-slave set up.

Gurus, high priestesses, mediums, cult leaders, spin doctors, life coaches, astrologers, religious leaders and therapists may all promise salvation. But if this comes from elsewhere, then that is where we stay – outside our true self. These guides may give us a fresh slant on life and expand our knowledge - their ideas can be so seductive and exciting, especially when they counteract laws and structures which were laid down for us in childhood. Yet while it is essential that our primal messages are questioned, who can we really trust?

We are no longer children, dependent on being cared for on condition that we act a certain way. We cannot please everyone. Indeed, however carefully I try to couch my ideas here, it is impossible to cover everyone's tender spots and needs. I am bound to offend. Also, there are always exceptions and additions to any principle. We have a mind of our own and we owe it to our self to use it. Therefore, rather than take on ideas from outside in blind faith, mine included, we need to collate, sift and sort many seed thoughts for ourselves.

Extricating what is true for me has not been easy, having never been encouraged to think and feel for my self. Initially, when I went inside, I found little there. Finding what I was not, however, enabled me to find out who I was and could be. Now, whatever happens, no one can take away the truth which comes from my experience of selfhood. On this I can forever expand - the antithesis of the void. It is the cause I cherish above all else in life.

As in the natural world, a fundamental principle is to plough back essential elements. Thereby we keep regenerating and cultivating a rich and balanced diversity, a deity on earth. Each of us may rise from the ashes of our former self and find a creative calling into which we can grow.

Without exception, we all have something special to contribute. This becomes evident when we are in accord with our essence and not overly governed by what is extrinsic to our being. What we do and attract comes more naturally to us as our intrinsic gifts flow more easily, no longer being stifled by our superego's or another's limiting attitude.

If only our primary carer could have looked into our eyes and felt, and shown, the wonder of us. Such windows would have kept us open to soul. Qualities and talents particular to us, would have flourished from the start. But do not give up. A wellspring of truly satisfying loving power still lies within. And if we should take care of any children, here is our chance to redress the balance by focusing on their genuine needs. Our reward will come as they develop into self assured yet sensitively honest, loving and yet strong, adults.

There is a saying, *If you love something set it free; if it comes back, it's yours and will be yours; if it doesn't return, it was never yours to begin with.* We may long to give, even more than to receive, love for the pleasure it arouses in us.

∗

The most common desire is for another to provide us with the love we lack and for us to fulfill the same for them. When we are 'in love' or experience a sexual orgasm, boundaries conjoin. This blissful symbiotic state is similar to being in the womb, merged with our 'good mother' in early infancy or with the divine.

While sex is the perfect recipe for propagating the species, it can become the chief arbitrator of expressing love. Yet, contrary to popular belief, as the magic of romance wanes, emotional closeness has room to grow and to redefine a relationship, so that the original attraction and sexual passion is surpassed.

But if our sense of self depends on maintaining the original status quo of oneness, we will not want our partner to further individuate. Similarly, what was never accepted in our self will remain invested in the other. A partner is sometimes referred to as the 'other half'. If he or she does not fulfill this want for completion, we can become disillusioned with that person.

If male, we might see in another our more feminine energy, or *anima*, holding wisdom and love which we express only as desire. The trouble with this is that, when alienated from these qualities in our self, there is no common ground for wisdom and love to meet – neither within us nor with another.

If the *animus* or masculine energy of action were to unite with the feminine within us, a viable self would be created; one which holds the potential to share the full spectrum of life energies with another. The old macho image might be foregone in the 'new male' but his masculine powerful energy need not diminish, just because he no longer completely overrules the female. As men come into harmony with and respect their own feminine qualities, softer feelings and intuition can guide their masculinity. Each polarity helps the other to manifest and find external connections.

Likewise, the female no longer needs to use manipulative ploys with her male counterpart. Neither does she have to hide behind, nor channel her potency through, the male. Yet, while she may choose to give up her traditional role as sole nurturer of home, children and husband, she need not lose touch with her feminine power and sensitivity.

While it is natural to major in the qualities associated with our gender, life has a way of showing us that, instead of being dependent on finding our less dominant function outside, we need to develop this for our self. However, even if we choose to live alone, we still need someone to relate ourselves to as a mirror in which we can observe our blind spots and our changes. But we do not need that person to define us.

When two authentic selves meet, a healthy engagement can develop. A perfect match is a relationship which continues to deepen; one full of the challenges, troughs, passion and excitement of sharing the journey of self discovery. Where a couple utilises this creative tension, the principle that 'the whole is greater than the sum of the two parts' holds true. Integrity within a partnership will enrich and stimulate growth of both individuals.

If we feel steadfast in our power along with genuine love, we are happy. We are invigorated and our fear of not surviving dissolves. Rather than sacrifice our self out of duty or desperate need for love, we can afford to leave any abusive relationship. Or, we can stay out of loyalty and loving kindness, knowing that we are capable of standing up to any abuse if we wish.

Many of us are desperate for a meaningful relationship but are frightened of being extinguished by pain, shame and loss of love were we to open up. Instead of confronting the fear of aloneness, which can edge us nearer to the non being state, we stay in a negative relationship, held by an infant-like need.

Where each only 'loves' the part in the other that is willing to adapt to his or her own needs, the relationship is a sham. So long as we delude and deny our true self and allow others to further cripple us in this way, they will continue to be unloving - and that is good for no one. If we do not care for our self, others will take this cue and treat us accordingly. If we bow to others in fear of rejection and/or abuse, is that sincere loving?

To some extent, we all give in to, and project onto, others rather than face our shadow. A heartening thought is that, although raw emotions are bad for us when repressed and when released unawarely, their essence often holds a potential force for good. So often, secondary aggression is used to camouflage and ward off feeling deep-seated vulnerability. A psychotic outburst is generally a desperate attempt to release the extreme tension of a confining milieu. Our psyche is trying to make a connection, within our self and with another.

※

Of course, intimate relationships are built by self revelation, not through attacking the other. For instance, we may scream 'This home is a tip', or use sarcasm or passive aggression so that our housemate feels as 'rubbished' as we do and therefore goes off into a temper or sulk. Or, we may evoke a more productive and empathic response by saying, 'Please can you help me out as, having tried to make this home both comfortable and clean, I am feeling unappreciated'.

When we object in the spirit of loving our self to those who are hurting us, rather than from a place of fear, it may be challenging all round but this might open up a space for healing. By honestly and clearly expressing our needs, the unvarnished truth flourishes. Yet truth can hurt, as well as liberate, and unless harnessed with goodwill, it can be destructive.

When identified with an afflicted subpersonality, our perspective can be so limited that there seems no choice but to inflict pain, shame or fear. If we can disidentify enough, step back, we may be in two places at the same time, rather than be swinging helplessly from one extreme to another. With this amalgamation comes choice which, in our hands, provides a fulcrum between our conscience and our primitive forces. Thus any immediate strong reactions to a situation can be contained until such time as we have distilled these, with mindfulness, into coherent thoughts and manageable feelings.

We become aware of a multiplicity of feelings, thoughts, sensations, images and intuitions upon which we can draw. We are self conscious in a healthy way and we can observe more clearly what response really serves our well being. From this central point of self, communication will be clearer and so more effective. Miracles do happen, believe me.

I used to imagine that the synthesis of different aspects would make for a controlled and boring life. But as my once disparate elements become more cohesive, a sense of unpretentious freedom is growing inside. This gives me confidence to respond to life in a spontaneous, yet more voluntary, manner. Eureka!

I remember a fellow therapist whose shadow I perceived to be very different from my own. Her more loving elements were beginning to emerge and my hostile emotions were rising.

Yet there was a moment when these hitherto split and seemingly opposite feelings met between us and at this point of contact, a meaningful and mutual healing occurred. We exchanged a look which cut through our apparent difference to what we had in common. We satisfied our need to really see each other's essence, the longing for recognition of who we were – a special moment. There can be a healthy meeting of souls at this deep level.

The wonder is that we might feel this accord, say with a check-out lady at the supermarket, when we feel irritable and her friendly smile touches a soft spot in our heart. Or, it may be that we catch the eye of a screaming child on a train and there seems to be instant recognition. A simple acknowledgment, a lovely rare gift, maybe a peace offering, passes between us. The extraordinary can be found in the most ordinary exchange and vice versa.

*

We can, however, only be as honest as consciousness allows. A principle which strikes me is, 'How true is our "yes" if we cannot say "no"?' This begs the question - how true is our love if we cannot own our hate? Jung (1966) proposed that, *'Logically, the opposite of love is hate and of Eros, Phobos (fear); but psychologically it is the will to power.'* Freud (1920) identified our instinct for life with the goddess of love, Eros, who sought and maintained relationship with others. He deemed the opposing force, Thanatos, our instinct for death, to be the destroyer of those connections.

An infant's innate sexuality and aggressive instinct is often deemed sinful and his naivety as good. But innocence can be the pretender of ignorance and we are ideally born, having both soft yet vigorous qualities. These come as a bundle of instinctual drives with which to make a loving connection with our primary carer - and with our self. Were we to enter the world loving others to the complete detriment of ourselves, we would not survive.

'Where love reigns, there is no will to power; and where the will to power is paramount, love is lacking.' (Jung, 1966) Although our many strands of emotion and urges are interdependent, they

so often are split. Here lies the challenge. If we do experience opposites operating at the same time, our means of feeling consistent can be cancelled out. This obscuration is what terrifies us most. It threatens annihilation, from where psychoses arise.

I had to grapple long and hard with my murderous agents before I found that, what is seemingly destructive is valuable also - it holds an impulse for creative change. Each pole might enliven, rather than cancel out the other. When extreme psychic energies surface and then each subtle variant is coordinated within a boundaried self, the deep primal split may heal. By uniting our love of self with our will to manifest that self within the heart centre, we become whole hearted.

It seems to me that I have had a change of heart - one more like the life-giving organ I was born with. As with a pivotal point of a pendulum, despite having swung far from my centre, it held true.

There are many life-changing practices and mystical pursuits which reframe suffering, dissolve personal difficulties and soothe the primal wound. Some find that linking to the divine relieves the anxiety, maybe intolerable terror, of a lack of identity. Others find that getting high on recreational drugs makes them feel full of the magnificence of mankind.

By going to the top before plumbing the depths, however, we will not develop a solid enough base below to bring our rarefied experience down to a manageable level. The heavenly stream of pure power and love might flow over us. But rather than this constellate within a true centre, we become lost in it. There is an illusion of strength but, having crossed the frontiers of the transpersonal realms, the superego will demand ever more shiny coats of perfection are applied, while the core self remains dying. When we have seen the light before including the dark, have transcended rather than have transformed, the residue of early wounding becomes more malignant.

✱

Madness can be the creative chaos in which such absolutes are freed as boundaries between mysticism and our early developmental issues overlap. The greatest 'con-fusion' is when we are between worlds and have no grasp on what is false and what is true. In psychosis, every sense, drive, thought and emotion from the genetic and universal unconscious, personal memory and potential future, vividly arrive together. It is all there, although it may take many years for our psyche to assemble these elements into a really stable self and new world order.

When we are at the depths of madness, we are at the apex of life's learning curve. But in order for there to be a viable relationship between the different dimensions, we need to rework our expansive psychotic experiences by interfacing with a therapist, so that we contract these forces into something with a more normal form. Our therapist can act as a self object and as a bridge between the ineffable, both horrific and beatific, while we become bound to our own sense of self existence. Struggling with our many raw, paradoxical elements, ultimately may result in a strong and flexible body and mind. Thus our soul will be securely anchored in the mortal world so that we can go soaring in safety into the spiritual domain.

Usually, when referring to the unconscious, depth is associated with the dark, threatening and 'bad' qualities, whereas height suggests light and love. Our essential purity and goodness to which we might aspire is often called our *higher self*. Journeying into the sky brings a sense of expansion, whereas going underground feels constricting. Yet by constriction we expand in the way that we are squeezed along the birth canal only to breathe out for life to enter.

So I found it was with my psyche. In an attempt to cut off from intense, difficult feelings, I had taken only small breaths in life. In psychosis all was stretched to the limit. I felt the pull from the darkest, annihilating, densest as well as lightest rarefied energies.

Thus the psychotic part of a person contains the soul as well as an extremely persecutory dyad. (Schwartz-Salant, 1989)

Feeling threatened by extinction, I opened my core wound wide until my heart made room for copious amounts of essential matter. Dynamic forces surged upwards from the fiery psychotic furnace. By going back to basics, love could flow, along with envy, shame, rage and smouldering resentment which had made it jaundiced and hatred which had made it freeze.

The profound transformation which might occur at this level liberates a self-generating energy which takes us into a fresh and wondrous world. Having found that we can trust the wisdom of our psyche in its unfoldment through psychosis, we may be sure of a guiding presence which can lead us into the sacred mysteries of life. Indeed, we may sense more fully that we are under the wing of a power that is greater than our personal will.

For my self, I have gleaned enough to tentatively believe that we come from and return to a collective source; that each is born with a precious and unique part of soul which can become one whole through us being fully incarnate in this world. Therefore, unless our primal forces were assimilated in childhood, we might have to regress to progress, disintegrate to integrate this raw material into a substantial self. Soul making means going down to our roots to find our original intention so that we can grow up naturally into the light of the world.

The quintessence of a really strong human is to be able to draw on a full spectrum of feelings, including vulnerability, and not be taken off balance. Real power can be measured by how love manifests, towards self and others. Regressing to the chaotic, instinctual forces of the infant may bring us back to life as a powerful being; a self who is really able to love and who feels truly lovable.

∗

Chapter 9

An Emergence Of Our True Self

We keep finding our self a little more each day.   Bach, 1972

When we have harnessed our psychotic forces we can safely swim, surf and splash about in psyche's emotional waves. We know and love, can express, and enjoy being, who we really are.

If all this sounds too good to be true, then I wish I could hold my self up as a shining example of its veracity. It would be great, and neat, to end this account of my journey to find my innermost being, by displaying the glorious trophy. I am living proof, however, that finding your self through madness is possible. For while the real me is not flourishing in all its fullness, quite yet, I know in every fibre of my body that I am coming to life with more of me than I have ever had before.

In the past chapters, while tracing a way through a psychotic landscape, I have mapped the pitfalls where we can become held fast by marauding entities, and the grave area where the body, the bastion of our psyche, may experience mortal peril. I have marked situations where vital drives can be quenched by palliative means and highlighted signs which indicate a passage to freedom.

Still questions remain and some posed are not fully answered. Yet no matter what is missing here, if bound for the psychic depths, whatever preparations made beforehand and whatever guidance received while there, your way would be different to mine. The result may be similar, however.

I know a few people who have bountifully matured by venturing into psychosis. Such individuals are not immediately recognisable as they are not walking around glowing with self satisfaction and serenity. It is more by their quality of contact that we can know them to be who they are. What they say, they mean and they truly 'walk their talk'. Not surprisingly, this genuine openness can be quite daunting to anyone used to subterfuge and innuendo. Yet they have a generosity of spirit, a live and let live attitude which is endearing, infectious, freeing and ultimately reassuring. To this I aspire.

*

Yet while my innate self still lives with some uncertainty and disregard, I used to despise this small, vulnerable being, as the following accounts will portray.

Six months before my psychotic episodes began, I was rummaging around in a cupboard when I came across a life-sized baby doll, a present from my mother when I was a child, which was stuffed inside a plastic bag. I was curious since just grasping the bag felt abhorrent.

I therefore took the package to my next therapy session - but never opened it - and to the next, and the next ... until one day my therapist did not answer my knock at his clinic door. There I stood outside transfixed, feeling utterly distraught and abandoned, until my hour was up. By this time all hope had gone and I fled, forgetting the bag.

The following session, my therapist apologised for his absence and explained that he had been in a car accident. Then he pointed out my doll, which I still had not missed. But I could not turn and look, such was my shame and disgust.

Each time I entered my therapist's room thereafter, I was to catch a glimpse of the doll sitting on his couch and feel quite aghast that he could tolerate its presence. I thought it was as pathetic as it was grotesque.

Yet he had taken in this foundling, a symbol of a vital part of me which got lost when I was little. Quite unconsciously I had re-enacted this abandonment. At the time I thought that I loved my therapist, whereas the reality was that I was infatuated. Therefore, rather than him speaking fond words which I would misconstrue, his gesture left room for purer and baser emotions to come to the fore.

So as time passed I perceived something very subtle was happening. His simple and sustained demonstration of kindness, although symbolic, felt almost tangible - an early sign that a connection might be possible.

But I was not yet ready to accept all of what my doll represented. Its eyes were closed and its white dress was covered in garish paint splotches. (It had been the central prop in a horror movie my daughter had made at art college – this damaged self surely had been passed on.) Thus it stayed on the couch for many months, ignored by me, until my therapist had to put it back in its bag for me to take home as he was moving premises.

A year or so passed before I took out the doll, very tentatively, and nestled it amongst some cushions in my cane swing chair. There it remains to this day. Its eyes have gradually opened and recently, I gave it a fresh dress. I even feel, at this point, like calling it 'she'.

*

Some five years later, my psyche conjured up a more evident sign that life was coming into my core self. This time, psychotic elements coalesced into a Biafran child sitting on my therapist's settee. I had no desire to hug this emaciated being – a discarded waif-like skeleton. Nothing but horror came from me. While this unwelcome visitor seemed only too life-like, just the notion of getting close was enough for her to collapse into dust and for my breath to blow away what was left of her.

Having lived in Nigeria during the Biafran war, I know how pictures of children, such as she, were used to elicit much needed funds. Although civil war exacerbated the plight of Nigeria's children, such is the poverty, and occasional brutality, in this country that some babies have been purposefully maimed – their legs or arms broken by their parents as a life-long source for begging.

Such means of using children, as fodder for our basic and basest needs, continue to be practised also in so-called more civilised society, although generally, the methods are more sophisticated and covert. Until we integrate our primal forces and grow more loving towards our neglected being, we will continue to abuse others, particularly vulnerable children, for our own ends.

My therapist was not fazed by my disaffection towards my ravenous child. Instead, he simply accepted this frail, seemingly unreachable, imaginary child. A warm caress can come as cold comfort if starving; rich food can choke or bring unbearable pain if consumed.

After half a century held in darkened captivity, this forgotten being was letting me know of its existence by externalising. Both replicas, the doll and wraith-like victim of war, I had seen as horrifying and repulsive. However, since my therapist could accommodate her, so she might stay in my sight and mind. Although devoid of any loving feeling, I sensed that I was starting to take custody of my orphaned child.

It seemed as if all the psychic fragments and traces which had passed between he and I over the years and the currents of emotion we were sharing in the present, were gathering in the field and forming a third entity. I was coming into closer contact with this estranged being - yet I could not tell, as she could not, what was pleasurable or painful. She was still neither in, nor completely out of, touch with life.

I knew something was there. But it was an indefinable mute being which could only tolerate quiet attention. Indeed, the most treasured time was when I experienced my therapist's willingness to just be there, even when I remained unable to respond. Any subtle encouragement, minute deviation or slight inflection would break the connection. An undemanding presence was 'all' that was needed at this juncture.

The wonder of being truly cared for as an infant is that we might see in another's eyes that we are lovable. The same goes for any subsequent attempt at self emergence. Only slowly did I deduce that, primarily, a form was coming into definition by my gradually adjusting to and meeting my therapist's eyes. My undeveloped self was being revealed to me, little by little, when I stayed in the present reality, without anticipating my past being repeated or expecting any particular new way of being. It all depended on my therapist remaining with me and being open to whatever may, or may not, emerge.

I would circle round this meeting place like a wild animal desperate to drink from a watering hole but terrified of attack. Could my glimpse of salvation be merely a mirage in the desert or was it a true reflection, a mirror of the fount within? It seemed tantalisingly near, yet it would disappear in a blink of an eye. For how could I sustain something which had never glowed brightly enough for me to see it in the first place? The person I was no longer existed and my true identity still seemed intangible and elusive. So who was I?

*

Eventually, all who became alienated from their essential self in childhood may come close to the void - that desolate place with an invisible edge. Some might border on non being in severe depression, others when in prolonged periods of dissociation and depersonalisation or if grief takes them drowning into the underworld. But inherent resources may first need to be liberated, flung far and wide in madness, before the central core can reveal itself fully.

Psychotic illusions reach beyond the ends of the world as we know it. Without any effective defence structure, anything might happen. We may oscillate between clinging on for dear life, as if to mother in total dependency, and spiralling down into our own, generally terrifying world and cut off from all living beings. In the boundlessness of madness, one minute any distance between self and other is disregarded; the next, psychotic entities take over and form a steel encasement so that there is not even this nebulous contact. We are encapsulated in hell or cast out into the ether.

However, we might be so absorbed in these dimensions that we become conditioned, almost hooked on such extreme ways of existence. Having come to be identified with the fathomlessness of water, the purgation and purification in fire and the elevation in air - we have little contact with matter. We may have 'lost it' in psychosis but we have found an extraordinary way of being.

In madness there can be a huge explosion of intensely charged impulses such as we have never felt before. All the shock waves blast as one. The adrenaline is running high and we feel as if we are battling for our life. But until such titanic forces have dazzled and battered our senses so that former adaptations have lost their hold, we will not drop down to the bottom of the unfathomable well of psychosis from where true aliveness springs.

At the end of a radical breakdown, we may try in vain to take up each once familiar place and angle, only to realise that all has been obliterated. This is when we are prone to a resurgence of madness as a deterrent to facing our uncertain future. Perhaps psychosis gave us the attention we craved. We could have played the drama queen, if our needs were ignored or trammelled in infancy. There again, maybe in our ravaged state we were vilified, shunned or stomped on, yet again, so we tried to hide away. The anticlimax hits hard regardless. So what happens now? We cannot go back to how we once were and moving forward into the unknown feels so terrifying and dangerous.

*

I felt a chilling sense of loss after all my psychotic manifestations died down. Despite there being no clean break from these perturbing episodes - they simply lessened and the periods of remission lengthened - the relative stillness was unnerving in a different way. Having been in the thick of it, now I was slipping in and out of 'nothingness' and of 'nobodiness'.

The world as I knew it was no more. It was as if I had fallen through a trap door into an alien state which was deadly silent and devoid of any meaning. Psychosis disfigures and lays waste everything in its path and like the tsunami, devastation remains. Without a fixed point or any coordinates from which to get my bearings, my sense of existence was not affirmed and neither was any movement. All I was left with was the stupefying awe which abounds a horrific catastrophe.

Beyond psychosis, there were no more illusions and diversions. Thus I moved from saturation point to emptiness. I reached unknowing and despair. In this state of flux I had nothing left other than the experience of non being. However insistent my urge for some kind of self attachment, there was nothing to hold onto, not even the surges which had once supercharged my body when I flipped from hyper excitation to collapse.

Following the stampede of psychosis, everything was swallowed up into a dark hole. Thereby I returned to the inception of soul; to the non-state before I knew my union to and separate existence from mother; to when my psychic awareness seemed suspended in endless time and space.

Some might say that there is nothing in a void because where there is an undefined space, then we have no sense of anything being there. But there is. Just as there is dark matter in our universe which, to date, has no scientific handle, so lying dormant in a psychic pool are the undiscovered elements which make up the core of our true self, yet to be created.

I could but stay, hovering betwixt doom and redemption, waiting for my inchoate self to come into form in its own sweet singular way. After the tumult of psychotic episodes, it was here in the existential nothingness that the process of embodying really began. Each body cell had remembered the sensory pangs of the original loss of self. A surety of my real identity was indeed incubating within me, biding its time until I felt a quickening, which heralded my rebirth.

But for now, into the fringes of awareness were trickling the distillations left from my psychotic elements; these finest of emotional threads which were to be woven into a new psychic framework for holding my burgeoning self.

The delicate evolvement of the core self into a fully functioning being can be likened to the transformational process of the caterpillar in its later stages. First the caterpillar eats its cabbage up, like all good children do. Then it spins a chrysalis, the protective adapted self, before dissolving into pulp, as in psychosis, which subsequently transforms into a butterfly.

But not so fast - following the butterfly's emergence, there is a limbic state when its gossamer wings hang, drying. These cannot unfold until there has been a period of quivering. In this prelude, the butterfly gradually realises its power and may only then, spread its wings and fly.

I had dissolved and there was much quivering. Throughout life, my soul had been waiting in the wings for me to come into harmony with the vibrational laws of my nature. But I could only settle ever so slowly into my self and from this centre gently radiate out into the wide unknown.

*

I do not remember the context of the therapy session in which a more fulsome recognition came, but this time I felt the primitive being within me, although it still had little substance. For a glorious moment, I felt truly alive. Now I had a connection, however tenuous, to who I was before being taken over by my carers and becoming frozen in time – and that felt so good. I belonged in this world. My psyche had reached beyond the psychotic layer, into the dumbness and numbness which had separated me from my enduring core being.

Although totally new in one way, it seemed as if I was coming home. Like a tender meeting with a long lost friend, it had an air of a tryst, a kept promise which came as a rippling wave of recollection. A calm feeling of rightness and well being flowed in this truly defining moment.

Now I really knew that I was born with a core self. Until then, it had been something I had only heard about and seen reside in others but never had the experience of. This was for real. But it was not a case of 'Hey presto, I've got it!', commonly called an 'aha' experience. Neither was it an expansion of consciousness such as when we see the sacredness of another human being or we are struck by the wonder of the universe. Out of nothing came something, so precious to me.

Despite this and after all that I had been through, any tentative effort to come back into the world in my true form still seemed fraught with danger. The expectation was that I would be rebuffed, ignored, violated or demolished. Although I was on the brink of a new life, waves of shame and fear again covered me just when I was at the point of becoming visible. The slightest encouragement to emerge sent my elusive elemental self ever deeper into the dark and it seemed that I was playing an endless game of 'hide and seek', so loved of little ones.

In truth, this inchoate being kept turning away as it could only come into existence by making me feel the longing and suffering it had endured in being parted from me. It was so. I could do nothing but trust this process.

It could not transpire until I could be still in uncertainty. In my hopeless and helpless state, I might only stay alert to what was coming into being – that which was always inside me but remained hidden and uncherished. Only in this mode of acquiescence would this forsaken being feel its way towards me. Although barely imperceptible, so rarely captured in the moment, the new synthesis of body, mind, feeling and spiritual self was to develop out of the nether space.

※

Nothing is everything. In order to grow strong you must first sink your roots deep into nothingness and learn to face your loneliest loneliness. (The unknown author of this passage will be acknowledged in any future edition of this work)

Making contact with the nascent self cannot be rushed - so many times we need to hear this. With the formation of a really bright star, initially, only pin pricks of light might be seen although their beam stretches to infinity. Thus if we wait patiently, through the empty silence we may feel a soft pulse which seems to harmonise with something long forgotten. It is only here in the barren transitional time, between madness and a new form of true sanity, our core self might come to us, a seed at a time. As in the life-death-life principle of renewal, out of a wasteland a fresh living landscape can grow – one where we can thrive in our own true way.

It takes many returns to the terrifying emptiness for it to become the meditative stillness in which the new arises – a sought after inner sanctum. The core self born out of the seemingly unbearable pre-personal space allows entrance to the trans-personal – from before to beyond – and back to the middle way from where one might just wait and see what happens.

The more that we come from a place of authenticity, the more self accepting and visible we become. In succouring our self, we are self perpetuating and our senses revel in this infinite resource. From here we might safely tap our spirituality and continue seeking enlightenment as our soul strives to conjoin with others.

Put this way, the process sounds rather trite and formulaic, whereas there are no short cuts to freedom and self realisation. Neither is it a direct progression and nor do we ever reach nirvana. Moreover, I found that having faced such cataclysmic forces, no hero's welcome awaited me on my return, as in myths and legends. Tales of tyrants and typhoons in distant lands are exciting to hear about. But few of us want to know about monsters which also inhabit our own back yard and those dangerous elements which lurk in our personal shadows.

While there is a risk of ridicule in the telling of outlandish exploits and esoteric odysseys, they remain sources of wonder, whereas discussing madness, particularly in regard to one's own, is generally considered taboo. But a mere mention of non being will bring a diabolical response, or not surprisingly, a blank look. Such talk threatens our perception of our finite form. In sharing with another the chilling formlessness which exists beyond active psychosis, we are confronting the ultimate boundary of humanity. The nihilistic place remains an area which is inconceivable and beyond common reasoning.

Each endeavour to engage with life warrants respect, including the creativity and fortitude needed to defend the deep narcissistic wound. But while a voyage of discovery to source might involve losing everything striven for, it is more vilified than glorified as in overt self sacrifice. Yet surely the search for wholeness is worthy of praise and honour, as an expression of our divinity.

Although we might always bear the scar of a narcissistic wound, where there's a will, however tired and torn, there may be a way to reach our deepest being. Indeed, while the focus has been on our true self's enfeeblement, its spirit of survival has transpired discreetly through this book - and it is time to exult in this.

*

Way down at a subsistence level, our core may still be found like a crystal embedded in a rock. Psychosis holds both the challenge and impetus to manifest what is most alive and real in us and therapy is a setting in which this may be held and honed into a precious jewel. In the awesome spaciousness beyond madness, we may finally rest, as in our mother's arms, so that our pure facets are constellated. There is no sweeter reward than when we sense self is at one with soul. It is the ethos and beauty which underwrites the disturbing nature of exploring psychosis.

We may reunite with what we perceive our source to be. We might find our self's meaning through madness so that our soul may be embodied in life. After all, if we lost our way back in infancy, we are hardly going to discover our self hiding in anything other than an abnormal reality. Madness slips into the ineffably spiritual and back to what is the base profundity of the human soul. Such might be the journey to wholeness.

Many hold the idea that we return from whence we came and that a newly born soul, just as one prior to death, is close to this source. But while we cannot be sure that our consciousness continues in some form when we leave this world and that we reunite with a greater source of power, it seems that some intrinsic elements go through a dying process when neglected in childhood. In which case, a way back to life may be through the 'dark night of the soul'.

When the light dawns that we cannot find lasting fulfillment from without, then we may surrender in this search and rediscover what resides within. We may uncover a secret, a vision of truth which we can no longer deny. The demands can seem formidable but the rewards are infinite and once we begin to appreciate this, then there is no turning back - so I have found.

Our life may appear quite mediocre so that we pass unacclaimed, our star might shine brightly yet still not be recognised in the eyes of the world - but we know who we are and that realisation and power cannot be taken from us.

And the end of all our exploring
Will be to arrive where we started
And to know the place for the first time. (Eliot, 1995)

Just as self fulfillment may sound too good to be true, we may also ask whether the only way to finding our self is through the psychotic realms, as it sounds too bad to be true. Rest assured, the primal wound may be tended to without going to such extreme measures. There are many levels of healing. It is for each one to decide – you alone can make this commitment. It may not be the right time for you just now. But if one day you do venture forth, your way may be safer than mine, having read my account, and your long lost self might come to you more readily.

Certainly I can testify that when we take on our inner demons, it is an awesome time. But so is the moment when we contact the undeveloped being which has stayed hidden inside us for so many years – a tiny miracle. The deathly void which is harboured by madness becomes the place of our birth and gives reason for rejoicing. Indeed, a little dose of madness may do us the world of good.

*

Glossary

alter ego — Secondary or alternative self.

anima — Personification of feminine characteristics, behaviour and modes of perception within the male.

animus — Personification of masculine characteristics, behaviour and modes of perception within the female.

archetype — Innate, primordial psychological model or image of instinct which influences mankind's functioning, being a component of the *collective unconscious*.

autistic — Psychoanalytical term for state of withdrawal from others due to mutual failure to connect. Psychiatric condition of undifferentitation where there is withdrawal into oneself, problem with language, fear of social interaction, resistance to change.

basic perinatal matrix — Term coined by Grof (see Bibliography) for stages in delivery of baby.

bipolar affective disorder — Intermittent or ongoing mood disorder fluctuating from phases of severe *depression* to *mania*.

body work — Therapeutic softening of the body's muscular holding patterns to gain access to deeply buried emotions or therapeutic strengthening to contain them.

borderline — Pertaining to traits found in a person operating through primary processes and primitive defence

	systems. One on the border between reasonable mental functioning and profound psychic disability due to an enfeebled self structure.
boundaries	Actual or imaginary holding structures which separate and distinguish one from another - as in time, space and people. Also the distinction between conscious thoughts and emotions, and those repressed.
brain stem	Area of brain associated with fundamental survival and body coordination. From this original structure has grown the cerebrum and cerebellum where higher mental functions such as interpretation and control of sensory inputs and action occur. See reptilian.
catatonic	As in fixed muscular rigidity and trance like state of consciousness.
chakra	A centre of energy (*chi*). Each of the body's seven chakras correspond with an endocrine gland, the supplier of hormones which balance the physiological system. Term originating from Eastern spiritual and medicinal beliefs.
chi	Pure, invisible cosmic energy.
co-dependent	As in a complementary relationship where contents of one's *personal unconscious* are experienced as being in another, so negated in self.

cognitive behavioural therapy
    Therapy which focusses on clients modifying their psychic processing of negative attitudes towards their experiences, in order to change their subsequent behaviour.

collective unconscious
    Psychic field holding both the inherited instinctual and creative potential which influences the individual and world in general.

complex	Cluster of ideas and memories around a similar emotional charge or core feeling which effects adaptations of behaviour whether conscious or not.

cortex Outer layer of cerebrum brain containing over nine billion neurological cells.

countertransference Therapist's emotional response to a client. Can stem from the client recreating his early relationship experiences but might include the therapists's emotional debris from his own unresolved problems. If unconscious, this will cause psychic infection. Bringing into consciousness and scrutinising the countertransference facilitates inter and intrapersonal conflict resolution.

daimon Deemed to be a soul companion which holds our unique blueprint or kernel of character and can call and guide us to fulfill our destiny.

defence mechanism Generally compulsive, unconsciously motivated protective psychic operation against thoughts and emotions liable to threaten the integrity and stability of the bio-psychological state.

delusion Belief which is held despite evidence to the contrary.

depersonalisation Psychic objectification in which the self, sometimes the body, is observed as not belonging or as estranged. There is little sense of substance and reality.

depression Broad term describing feelings of sadness, hopelessness, helplessness, low self esteem, apprehension, guilt and lack of interest and effect in outside activities. Both psyche and soma can shut down.

differentiation Psychic development beyond the basic or primal condition through separation and identification of individual sensations, intuitions, emotions, thoughts from whole, which gives conscious access to psychological functions.

dissociation Act or result of operating from a separate set of emotions, thoughts, behaviours while consciousness is cut off from other parts of the psyche or soma which might cause anxiety.

dissociative identity
Psychological disorder where loss of integrated conscious functioning, self perception and sensory mechanisms is extended.

drives
Internal energetic motivational forces which include instinctual biologically determined and psychic urges. Primary drives associated with food, water, sex, pain, avoidance etc are universal.

ego
Psychic formation which tries to maintain a balanced psychic organisation by mediating the basic drives, dealing with stress and through cognitively relating to the outer environment, the self and *superego*. Similar to the term the 'adapted self' as it does not include what is unconscious.

electroconvulsive therapy
Procedure of passing weak electric currents through the brain of severely depressed patients to induce seizure.

E.M.D.R.
Eye Movement Desensitisation Reprocessing therapy, which suggests that eye movements can reduce the intensity of disturbing thoughts and feelings under certain conditions.

encephalitis-lethargica
Inflammation of the brain or brain membranes causing lethargy and prolonged periods of sleeping.

Eros
The Greek god of love who Freud related to life preserving, including sexual, instincts.

exclusion factors
Adverse characteristics, modes of behaviour, also insufficient factors such as social support structures, strength of will and *self*, intellectual capacity – all of which indicate a person's inability to benefit from working with a psychotherapist or psychoanalyst.

false memory syndrome
Recovered information from the unconscious

which is reconstructed rather than reproduced. This disparity is due to how psychological material from the past is stored in such a way that it is susceptible to being reformulated into associations which are inaccurate. Term coined with particular reference to unproven memories from adults of sexual abuse in childhood.

false self   The self who has compliantly developed out of a need to be acceptable or as a reaction against the pressure of the primal environment, in order to survive. It covers our true needs and potential. (Winnicott, 1960a & 1965) See *self*.

field   Psychological space wherein dynamic configurations and interactions, conscious and unconscious are present.

flashback   Spontaneous replay of a disturbing experience. People feel they are back in the moment as all sensations, thoughts and emotions can be restimulated.

folie a deux   Meaning 'insanity in pairs'. Two people exhibit the same mental disturbance together.

force-field   Field of ions, free electrons and protons surrounding a solid physical body as a result of chemical processes within. (Western version of the aura)

fragmentation   Loss of continuity and cohesion of psyche thus of sense of identity.

fusion   When separate elements such as life/death, self/other, love/hate cannot be perceptually differentiated.

Gestalt   Therapy formulated by Fritz Perls which includes the technique where the client switches between two empty chairs to act out both sides of a dialogue in an attempt to resolve conflicting feelings with two aspects of himself or with another person.

good enough mother
   One who recognises and responds sufficiently to

the child's real needs without superimposing her own. Such a carer facilitates the development of a healthy *narcissistic* sense of *true self* within the child.

guided imagery Procedure which encourages a client to image an experience, symbol or scene, a construction not necessarily a true reproduction, in order to evoke and/or transform emotions, thoughts and behaviour.

hallucination The perception of a sensory stimulus coming from an external object which is not actually present but is a representation of energy from something seemingly lost or buried within the unconscious.

higher self Spiritual, superconscious, transpersonal or universal self which includes the finest psychic functions such as intuition, altruistic love and will. It provides direction for a meaningful unfoldment and manifestation within the *true self*. Although transcending, paradoxically it is also to be found through the deepest elements as in *psychosis*.

inclusion factors Indicators of a client's propensity to a successful outcome from psychotherapy or analysis e.g. ability to reflect and make psychic links, empathise, take appropriate responsibility, have realistic self esteem and supporting milieu.

individuation Developmental process in childhood of disengaging from the primary carer in order to become a defined autonomous self.

integration Process of coordinating and modifying psychic and sensory elements into a whole system.

introjection Internalisation of other people's values, standards or traits, often in order to prevent conflicts with or threats from them, as with acceptance of attitudes of primary carer and society as one's own. Also assimilation of *self object* into *self*.

I-Thou Pertaining to a respectful relationship between

	two equal individuals, as opposed to one where a person is treated as an object, an 'it' to brace up the other's precariously constituted persona.
libido	Instinctual drive, life giving energy or sexual urge which includes the psychic impulse to satisfy desires.
L.S.D.	Lysergic acid diethylamide. A psychoactive drug capable of producing extreme alterations of consciousness.
liminal	Pertaining to the threshold between psychological stages where there are disorientating shifts of awareness.
mania	Pathological mental state when purposeless activity, inflated self esteem, high spirits, unfounded elation, distractibility, grandiose plans and need for stimulus run rife, in denial of unconscious feelings of loss and defeat in *depression*.
meridians	Invisible lines or channels along which *chi* energy flows in the body. Term of Eastern origin.
mirror	Person or act of reflecting back what is there to be seen in another and thereby the recipient might realise who they are.
narcissism	Freudian concept, named after the Greek god Narcissus (Grant & Hazel, 1973) who fell in love with his own image, where there is extreme investment, focus on self interest and continuing need for love of self image and esteem. This is a secondary formation when primary narcissism, a healthy love of self activated through the primary relationship, was not established in infancy.
narcissistic	Pertaining to traits found in a person attempting to procure from the environment self soothing support, admiration and love for their idealised persona or self image.
narcissistic wound	- see *primal wound*
neurosis/es	Part of the human condition of erecting defences against anxiety. In an extreme form, a

psychological disorder when a person has a very high level of anxiety but is still in reasonable contact with reality.

neurotic — Pertaining to the symptoms of and the person who exhibits *neurosis*.

non being — Terrifying state of feeling powerless, not real or existing which arises from the *self* being abnegated in infancy by the primary carer.

Oedipus — Name of king in Sophocles legend (Grant & Hazel, 1973) used by Freud for concept of conflictual childhood rivalry and jealousy of same sexed primary carer and wish for sexual possession of carer of opposite sex. Called the Oedipal *complex* in a male and the Electra *complex* in a female.

oral phase — Appertaining to regressed emotional response and behaviour which resembles the earliest developmental stage [0-1+yrs.] of sensating pleasure and aggression through tactile connection of the mouth to an object. Freud's term.

panic attack — Psycho-somatic response to an overwhelming dread which precipitates heart palpitations, sweating, difficulty in breathing, trembling and a feeling of unreality.

paranoia — General term for *delusions* of persecution or/ and grandiosity which can become a system of perception where self and others are split into wholly good or bad. Rather than multiple splitting or *fragmentation* persisting as in *schizophrenia*, a person suffering paranoia might continue to function normally in other areas.

passive aggressive — Behaviour where no overt aggression is shown. There is some obstructive indirect reaction, often unconscious, but little effective initiation of action.

peak experience — Moment when a person has little concern for time and space and experiences blissful harmony,

personal unconscious
oneness with the universe, a sublime 'high', clarity and spontaneity. The term was coined by Abraham Maslow and Fritz Perls.

personal unconscious
Individual's repository of repressed experiences.

phobia Sustained fear for something which is not objectively dangerous. Often object or situation feared is a symbol of a deeper unconscious fear which is displaced.

play space Place where time is freely allowed for the mastery of cognitive and behavioural skills. Winnicott's term from when an infant feels held safely without experiencing inhibiting demands from his primary carer.

pleasure principle
Uninhibited need to discharge psychic energy in order to reduce the tension of drives and gain satisfying balanced harmony within.

post traumatic stress disorder
Long-term after affects of a catastrophic experience which has shattered a person's sense of reasonable chance of survival. Symptoms include recurrent and intrusive disorder recollections and reliving the experience in *flashbacks* and dreams. There is hyperarousal and intense psychological distress from internal or external cues which stimulate such reactions.

primal forces Unbound, undifferentiated, unevolved basic energy, the pressure of which motivates activity. Fundamental and *primitive* urges for growth. Simplest units of sensory *drives* and emotions which have the potential to come into conscious therefore controllable form.

primal wound Lasting effects of early break in security and failure by primary carer to foster a true sense of *self* – also known as the *narcissistic wound*.

primitive Pertaining to the very early or archaic stage before development and *differentiation* of the psyche.

primordial Existing from the very beginning of time.
projection Automatic mental process of placing or ascribing in another one's own unacceptable urges, thoughts and emotions thereby externally objectifying what is denied subjectively.
psyche Used throughout text as the totality of all mental and emotional processes, conscious as well as unconscious. ref 'No.6. The Collected Works of C.G.Jung' & Samuels, Shorter & Plaut (1986) 'A Critical Dictionary of Jungian Analysis' London: Routledge
psychic Appertaining to the *psyche* i.e. not particularly to the paranormal.
psychoanalyst Person trained to help another utilise the communication and relationship in a session in order to release and modify psychopathological processes. Method of applying thought and interpretation to psychic processes in order to bring greater self awareness and through this freer choice of mood, perception, attitude and behaviour. Often the client is invited to recline in a position from which he need not observe the analyst. This lack of visual contact may reduce the client's conscious control therefore encourage verbal free association so there is optimum flow of repressed sensations, emotions and thoughts. While this position can reduce inhibiting *transference*, the frequency of sessions, between two and five per week over sometimes many years means that intense patterns of dependency needs might be activated and addressed. Many variables originating from Freud.
psychopathology Scientific study and arrangement of mental processes which may be cause of psychological disturbance. The word 'psychopathology' combines understanding (logos) the suffering (pathos) of the soul (psyche).

psychosis A serious breakdown of mental structures and functioning which brings altered and disturbing states of perception and belief without any concept of reality. With no effective defensive structure or awareness of distorted reality, the unconscious takes possession. When the condition persists it is classified as a psychiatric disorder i.e. paranoid *schizophrenia* and some mood disorders.

psychosynthesis Healing of the dysfunctional splits or *dissociations* of mind, body, feelings and spirit to form a potentially whole self. Roberto Assagioli founded the Psychosynthesis Research Foundation, developed and wrote on the practice of psychosynthesis.

psychotherapist Person trained to enable another person to utilise the communication and relationship within a session, in order to release and modify *psychopathological* processes; to bring greater awareness and through this freer choice of mood, perception, attitude and behaviour. The psychotherapist remains visible to the client and utilises the transference and countertransference more often than counsellors, many of whom do not focus on the dynamic therapeutic relationship. Generally sessions are once or twice a week.

psychotic Throughout the book referring to extremely regressed behaviour, emotions, sensations and thoughts and where the inner experience bears little resemblance to what is apparent in the outside world. Also a clinical term for severe psychic disorder diagnosed as psychiatric e.g. psychotic *depression*. Person diagnosed as suffering from *psychosis*.

reactive formation
Exaggerated counteraction/defence often diametrically opposed to a repressed trait which would cause anxiety e.g. shyness is counteracted by exhibitionism.

reframing	Means by which a different perspective is given to the one offered, generally turning something seen through a negative or distorted lens into something positive or clearer e.g. reinterpreting what is experienced as an obstacle into an opportunity for creative learning.
regression	Retreat under stress to earlier or more immature patterns of behaviour.
repression	Defensive psychic process of excluding from awareness distressing internal emotions, drives, ideas or wishes, although tension accumulates from their impulses. Repression is unconscious, suppression is conscious.
reptilian	Pertaining to basic primordial brain formation out of which adapted higher functions have grown. Aggression and territoriality are associated with this area.
retroflect	Pertaining to an unconscious hostile thought or impulse towards another person which is redirected towards oneself.
rogue kundalini	Sudden uncontrolled rise of repressed base energy through the *chakras* which results in physical, psychic and spiritual crisis or emergency. The unprepared or immature self is unable to contain the released, potentially illuminating material. See Nelson (1994) where madness is placed within both neuropsychiatry and Eastern philosophy.
sado-masochistic	Pertaining to person who blends pleasure with pain. The sadistic part directs aggressive or sexual drives outwards and the masochistic part inwards.
schizoid	Withdrawn and emotionally aloof.
schizophrenia	Umbrella term for *psychotic* disorders where there is continued splitting or *dissociation* of emotions and cognitive thoughts. Major disturbance in behaviour and faulty perception e.g. *delusions*, *hallucinations* and reduced tolerance to stress.

self The nuclear psychic core of person which gives a central continuing sense of order and meaning of his/her independent existence. When individual selfhood is not integrated in infancy the baby's *true self* goes underground and he presents to the world a coping and compliant *false self* experienced as emptiness, meaninglessness and inauthenticity. ref. Winnicott, D.W. (1958) 'Collected Papers: Through Paediatrics to Psychoanalysis' London: Tavistock and (1965) 'The Maturational Processes and the Facilitating Environment' London: Hogarth

self/constant object
  Person or object subjectively used and experienced by another as part of self, to provide a function of organisation, satisfaction, security, self esteem.

shadow Hidden aspects of person generally considered 'bad' so suppressed and those elements which were not recognised or accepted by primary carer so remain repressed in unconscious.

shaman A prophet and healer found in archaic cultures who mediates between society and the supernatural.

sociopath *Psychotic* individual who lacks or has limited anxiety for his anti social behaviour.

splitting Act of keeping incompatible feelings apart, often separating off a faction into the unconscious. Also viewing self and others as all good or all bad, as opposed to being a balance of positive and negative attributes.

subpersonality Semi-autonomous part of the *psyche* that operates out of its own *complexes* and traits which are organised around an inner drive. It is often inconsistent with and in conflict with other subpersonalities or aspects.

superego Internal controlling function which evaluates the self thus creating and reigning over the *ego*.

Formed in mid childhood out of the internal aggressive and creative forces, from the carers' prohibitions and ideals and also, in later life, from those of society. Can act as the conscience.

survivor persona Functional part of a person exclusively concerned with the relation to others. Generally formed early in life as an adaptation of the true individual self in response to the perceived demands of the primary carer.

symbiosis Interdependence between infant and primary carer where the fantasy is held that there is a dual entity within a common *boundary*.

tinnitus Experience of ringing in the ears when there is no defined external stimulus.

transference Designating patterns of emotion, thought and behaviour from past relationships onto present encounters; a living experience which can become conscious in the therapeutic situation. The therapist, as symbolic representation of primary carers, enables hitherto repressed conflicts to be examined in present reality.

transpersonal realms
External sphere from which instinctual, mystical, moral and aesthetic stimuli flow, influencing and inspiring the evolution of the individual and collective humanity.

true self Who in us feels genuine, spontaneous and whole. (Winnicott, 1960a & 1965)

unconditional positive regard
Attitude of one human being to another which exudes warmth, empathy, complete acceptance and total attention. (Rogers' term)

unifying centre Initially the primary carer who facilitates the connection to and flowering of the infant's true core self until this this function can be internalised by the child. Other significant people, causes or *archetypes* can take on this role of supporting the *self*. (Assagioli's term)

unipolar   Major disorder of *depression* without the phase of *mania* and likewise *mania* without subsequent *depression*.
vaginismus   Condition when vaginal muscles go into spasm preventing or inhibiting sexual intercourse.
wise being   Personification of inner wise guidance which facilitates the unfoldment of *self* potential.
wounded healer   Term which acknowledges the mutual healing dynamic that exists within the therapeutic relationship. Jung saw this *archetype* in the legend of a Greek doctor named Asclepius, who created a healing sanctuary for the wounded in recognition of his own wounds.

✶

Professional Bodies

The British Association of Psychotherapists
37 Mapesbury Road, London NW2 4HJ
Tel: 020 8452 9823 : www.bap-psychotherapy.org

The British Confederation of Psychotherapy
West Hill House, 6 Swains Lane, London N6 6QS
Tel: 020 7267 3626 : www.bcp.org.uk

The British Psycho-Analytical Society
112a Shirland Road, Maida Vale, London W9 2EQ
Tel: 020 7563 5000 : www.psychoanalysis.org.uk

United Kingdom Council for Psychotherapy
2nd Floor, Edward House, 2 Wakley Street, London EC1V 7LT
Tel: 020 7014 9977 : www.psychotherapy.org.uk.

✶

Bibliography

Bach, R. (1972) *Jonathan Livingston Seagull* UK: Turnstone Press
Barrie, J. (1988) *Peter Pan* London: Collins
Blake, W. (1993) *I Was Angry* from *The Rag and Bone Shop of the Heart* ed. Bly, Hillman, Meade. New York: HarperCollins Boadell, D. (1979) *The Charge Of Consciousness - Energy, chemistry and the dynamics of the brain* Zurich: Abbotsbury Publications
Brennan, B. (1988) *Hands of Light* and (1993) *Light Emerging* USA Bantam Books
Buber, M. (1958) 3rd ed. *I and Thou* transl. by W. Kaufman. Edinburgh: T. and T. Clark
Carroll, L. (1993) *Alice in Wonderland and Through the Looking Glass* London: Dent
Conger, J.P. (1994) *The Body in Recovery - Somatic Psychotherapy and the Self* Berkeley California USA Frog Ltd
Dante, A. (1998) *The Divine Comedy*, translated by C. H. Sisson, Oxford: Oxford University Press
Davison, G.C. & Neale, J.M. (1998) 7th ed. *Abnormal Psychology* USA John Wiley & Sons
Dickenson, E. (1992) *Much Madness is Divinest Sense* from *The Rag and Bone Shop of the Heart* ed. Bly, Hillman, Meade. New York: HarperCollins
Eliot, T.S. (1995) *Little Gidding - Four Quartets* London: Faber
Finn, C.C. (1966) *Please Hear What I Am Not Saying* Original version from www.poetrybycharlescfinn.com/Index.htm
Freud, S. (1920) *Beyond the Pleasure Principle* vol. 18 London: Hogarth
Grant, M. & Hazel, J. (1973) *Who's Who: Classical Mythology* London: J M Dent
Gribbin, M. & J. (2003) *The Science of Philip Pullman's His Dark Materials* London: Hodder Children's Books
Grof, S. (1985) *Beyond the Brain* New York: State UNYP
Jimenez, J.R. (1973) *I Am Not I* translated by Robert Bly from *Selected Poems of Lorca and Jimenez* Boston, USA Beacon Press

Jung, C.G. (1946) *The Psychology of the Transference* vol.16. of Collected Works. Princeton University Press
Jung, C.G. (1956) *Symbols of Transformation* vol. 5. of Collected Works. London: Routledge and Kegan Paul
Jung, C.G. ed. Jaffe, A. (1963) *Memories, Dreams, Reflections* London: Collins and Routledge and Kegan Paul
Jung, C.G. (1966) *Two Essays on Analytic Psychology* vol. 7 of Collected Works. London: Routledge
Karen, R. (1998) *Becoming Attached - First Relationships and How They Shape Our Capacity to Love* Oxford: Oxford University Press
Keenan, B. (1992) *An Evil Cradling* London: Random House
Kelley-Laine, K. (1997) *Peter Pan; The Story of Lost Innocence* UK: Element Books
Kramer, P.D. (1996) *Prozac and Personality* from *Sacred Sorrows* ed: Nelson, J.E. & A. New York: Putnam's Sons
Laing, R.D. (1959) *The Divided Self: An Existential Study in Sanity and Madness* London: Tavistock
Little, M. (1981) *Transference Neurosis and Transference Psychosis* USA: Jason Aronson
McFadden, J. (2001) *Quantum Evolution: The New Science of Life* New York: HarperCollins
Melville, H. (1993) *Pierre: Or, the Ambiguities* from *The Rag and Bone Shop of the Heart* ed. Bly, Hillman, Meade. New York: HarperCollins
Miller, A. (1987) *For Your Own Good: The Roots of Violence in Child-rearing* London: Virago Press
Moore, T. (1992) *Care of the Soul* UK: Judy Piatkus
Nelson, J.E (1994) *Healing the Split: Integrating Spirit Into Our Understanding of the Mentally Ill* Albany New York: State University of New York
Nielson Chapman, B. (1997) *Sands and Water* New York: Reprise Records
Nietzsche (1969) *Thus Spoke Zarathustra* Harmondsworth UK: Penguin Books
Perls, F., Hefferline & Goodman (1972) *Gestalt Therapy* London: Souvenir Press
Redfearn, J. (1989) *The energy of warring and combining opposites: problems for the psychotic patient and the therapist in achieving the symbolic situation* Ch.10, *Psychopathology: Contemporary Jungian Perspectives* ed. Samuels, A. London: Karnac Books
Redfield Jamison, K. (1993) *Touched With Fire: Manic-Depressive Illness*

and the Artistic Temperament New York: Macmillan
Redfield Jamison, K. (1996) *The Unquiet Mind* London: Picador & Toronto: Random House
Redfield, J. (1994) *The Celestine Prophecy* UK: Bantam Books
Roethke, T. (1960) *In a Dark Time* from *The Collected Poems of Theodore Roethke* New York: Bantam Doubleday & Co.
Sacks, O. (1973) *Awakenings* London: Gerald Duckworth
Schweitzer, A. (1875-1965) *philosopher, physician, theologian, musician*
Schwartz-Salant, N. (1989) *The Borderline Personality: Vision and Healing* IL. USA: Chiron Publications
Sheldrake, R. (2003) *The Sense of Being Stared At* UK: Hutchinson
The American Psychiatric Association (1994) *Diagnostic and Statistical Manual of Mental Disorders (DSM IV)* Washington DC: American Psychiatric Association Press
Thoreau, H.D. (1993) *The Wild Mallard Thought* from *The Rag and Bone Shop of the Heart* ed. Bly, Hillman, Meade. New York: HarperCollins
Watts, G. F. (1886) *Hope* Oil on canvas displayed London: Tate Gallery and Compton, Surrey: Watts Gallery
Wilde, O. (1966) *The Complete Works of Oscar Wilde: Stories, Plays, Poems and Essays* UK: William Collins
Wilde, O. (1973) *De Profundis and Other Writings* New York: Penguin Books
Winnicott, D. (1960) *Ego Distortion in Terms of True and False Self* London: Hogarth Press
Winnicott, D. (1965) *The Maturational Processes and the Facilitating Environment* London: Hogarth Press
Winnicott, D.W. (1971) *Playing and Reality* London: Tavistock
Woolf, V. (1944) *Moments of Being* from *A Haunted House & Other Short Stories* New York: Harcourt

SUGGESTED GENERAL READING

Chapter 4. A Construct of Self

Assagioli, R. (1965) *Psychosynthesis: A Manual of Principles and Techniques* New York: Viking
Brown, B. (1999) *Soul without Shame* Boston, USA: Shambala Publishing

Cloke, W. (2001) *Rage, Shame and the Death of Love* (www.ProPsych.com/WCloke)
Firman, J. & Gila, A. (1997) *The Primal Wound* New York: State University of N.Y. Press
Karen, R. (1998) *Becoming Attached: First Relationships and How They Shape Our Capacity to Love* Oxford: Oxford University Press
Kaufman, G. (1992) *Psychology of Shame* London: Routledge
Parfitt, W. (2006) *Psychosynthesis: The Elements and Beyond* Glastonbury: PS Avalon
Miller, A. (1987) *The Drama Of Being A Child* London: Virago Press
Sunderland, M. (2006) *The Science of Parenting: Practical guidance on sleep, crying, play and building emotional wellbeing for life* London: Dorling Kindersley
Wellings, N. (2000) *The Wound* Ch.4 *Transpersonal Psychotherapy: Theory and Practice* ed. Wellings, N. and McCormick, E.W. London & New York: Continuum
White, A. (1996) *Going Mad to Stay Sane: The Psychology of Self-Destructive Behaviour* London: Gerald Duckworth & Co Ltd
Winnicott, D.W. (1971) *Playing and Reality* London: Tavistock

Chapter 5. A Formation of Repeating Patterns

Assagioli, R. (1967) *Psychosomatic Medicine and Bio-Psychosynthesis* New York: Psychosynthesis Research Foundation
Keleman, S. (1989) *Patterns of Distress - Emotional Insults and Human Form* Berkeley California USA: Center Press
McDougall, J. (1988) *Jung and Reich: The Body As Shadow* California USA: North Atlantic Books
McDougall, J. (1989) *Theatres of the body: A psychoanalytical approach to psychosomatic illness* London: Free Association Books

Chapter 6. A Perspective of Madness and Sanity

Davison, G.C. & Neale, J.M. (1998) *Abnormal Psychology* 7th ed. USA: John Wiley & Sons
Golomb, E. (1992) *Trapped In The Mirror: Adult Children of Narcissists in their Struggle for Self* New York: William Morrow and Co.
Hinshelwood, R.D. (2004) *Suffering Insanity - Psychoanalytic Essays on Psychosis* England, New York: Brunner-Routledge

Jacoby, M. (1990) *Individuation & narcissism: the psychology of self* in *Jung & Kohut* London, New York: Routledge

Kalsched, D.E. (2003) *Daimonic elements in early trauma* Journal of Analytical Psychology U.K.: Blackwell and (1996) *The Inner World of Trauma: Archetypal Defenses of the Personal Spirit* London & New York: Routledge

Lemma, A. (1996) *Introduction to Psychopathology* London: Sage Publishing

Miller, A. (1979) *Depression And Grandiosity As Related Forms Of Narcissistic Disturbances* Int. Rev. Psycho-Analytical Journal 6, 61

Samuels, A. ed. (1989) *Psychopathology: Contemporary Jungian Perspectives* London: Karnac Books

Sharp, D. (2001) *Digesting Jung - Food for the Journey* Toronto: Inner City Books

Chapter 7. An Empowering or Disempowering Therapeutic Holding

Assagioli, R. (1965) *Psychosynthesis: A Manual of Principles and Techniques* New York: Viking

Field, N. (1996) *Breakdown & breakthrough: Psychotherapy in a new dimension* London and New York: Routledge

Ford, Dr Clyde W. (1993) *Compassionate Touch* New York: Parkside

Rosenberg, J.L., Rand & Asay (1985) *Body, Self, & Soul - Sustaining Integration* Atlanta USA: Humanic Ltd

Sedgwick, D. (1994) *The Wounded Healer* London & New York: Routledge

Schwartz-Salant & Stein ed. (1986) *The Body in Analysis* USA: Chiron

Chapter 9. An Emergence of Our True Self

Martel, Y. (2002) *Life of Pi* UK: Canongate

Wellings, N. (2000) *Naked Presence* from *Transpersonal Psychotherapy: Theory and Practice* ed. Wellings, N. and McCormick, E.W. London & New York: Continuum

✻

Printed in the United Kingdom
by Lightning Source UK Ltd.
133858UK00001B/133/P